# Nothin' Like I Thought

## A Baby-Boomer's Look
## in the Rear View Mirror

*To Peg*
*Enjoy*
*Arlene Avery Burke*
*November 2007*

By Arlene Yvonne Avery Burke

# Nothin' Like I Thought

## A Baby-Boomer's Look
## in the Rear View Mirror

By Arlene Yvonne Avery Burke

emersonstreet books

Olympia Fields, IL

NOTHIN' LIKE I THOUGHT
A Baby-Boomer's Look in the Rearview Mirror

By Arlene Yvonne Avery Burke

Published by:
emersonstreet books
20185 Augusta Drive
Olympia Fields, Illinois 60461
Fax: 1-708-748-8531
e-mail: ayburke@emersonstreetbooks.com

Arlene Y. Avery Burke, Publisher/Editorial Director
Yvonne Rose / Quality Press, Editorial & Project Consultant
The Printed Page, Interior & Cover Design

ISBN#: 978-0-9794844-3-8 / 0-9794844-3-X

2nd Printing

# Dedication

*This book is dedicated to my parents,*
*James and "Boots" Avery who did a good job*
*and to my husband Sterling who inspired me to just do it.*

# Acknowledgments

Thank you to my girlfriends, the "voices" in this book and to my sister, my first girlfriend, for sharing their thoughts. Thank you to Eva Liljendahl, my "coach" and Rita Coburn Whack for their advice and council during the writing process.

# Contents

# Prologue

I thought I knew a lot about life…

I'm the middle child of a loving, two-parent, middle class African American family and I grew up in Evanston, Illinois. Evanston was a wonderful town despite its mostly segregated housing and schools at the time. My elementary school provided a high-quality educational foundation for me and my siblings. My mother stayed home with us, until my younger sister went to school full time. Our parents were hard working, supportive, protective and well educated. They both attended Langston University, completing about three years, until World War II disrupted things by drafting my father into the Navy. They married in 1939. My brother, Jim, their first child, was born in 1943. My sister and I followed three years apart.

Newspapers and magazines were delivered to our home and read on a regular basis. We took music and dance lessons; participated in scouting; summer camp and Jack and Jill; made trips to the library—except in summer when the "book mobile" traveled to our community. (Remember the book mobile? It was a long, brown truck full of books that drove through the neighborhood once or twice a month. We could board and browse for about thirty minutes before the driver left for the next neighborhood.) Our teachers had always challenged us to read a book a week over the summer. I tried and never quite achieved that goal.

My sister and I played the piano; my brother was more interested in the trumpet. Piano recitals used to scare me to death. I started each performance on the piano bench; and by the last note I was already on my feet in flight to my seat. I endured it for years. My sister, Marsha, was a natural. Music lessons were quietly encouraged.

On Sundays we attended Sunday school and church within walking distance from home; securing our near perfect attendance. All three of us attended college. It was expected. I was successful in achieving both BS and MS degrees. I have continued my educational pursuit through online courses and conferences; learning new ideas, techniques, technologies and strategies for the successful implementation of such. I have tried to honestly evaluate my shortcomings and supplement with the help of others as needed.

My husband and I have enjoyed full employment during adult life. We've traveled and networked with well-educated and successful people. I followed in my mother's footsteps becoming a member of both Delta Sigma Theta Sorority and The Links Incorporated. I am able to communicate and work with people of various ethnic, cultural and religious backgrounds. I have played the game fairly and cautiously, to minimize mistakes and not squander opportunities. I was very well prepared for life...I thought.

It's easy to see life from your own circumstance or point of view. I thought if I emulated my parents' child rearing practices, with my children, I would achieve like results. I thought if you teach children right from wrong, they will choose to do the right thing. I thought hard work would always be rewarded. I thought people who asked, really wanted to hear the truth. I planned to marry and become a housewife, working part time just for fun. What made me think that would ever be my reality? I knew my parents couldn't live forever, except I didn't know how much I would miss them once they were gone. I couldn't have guessed that my children would come to me and not through me. I was unprepared for the level of dishonesty, greed and hatefulness that exists in this world. I thought people who professed to be Christian would behave as such. Who would have thought that when I turned fifty, I would be fifty pounds heavier than the day I married? I tried to be a good person, a loving wife, a loyal sister, a kind daughter, a generous friend, but the older I get, the more I realize, I DON'T KNOW JACK…and that's what this book is about.

As I approached fifty, I started to question where my life had been and what I would do with the rest of it. I heard myself saying, "Is this it?" "Is this all there is?" "Have I played it too safe?" "Is there time to do something I have only dared to dream about doing?" "What have I done?" "What legacy will I leave behind?" "What will endure once I am gone?" I realized that some of my aspirations and dreams had not come to fruition, and most probably never would. As I broached this subject with my friends, I discovered that I was not alone in my thinking. Everyone has some baggage – misunder-standings, guilt, pain, resentment, regrets, disillusionment, unresolved conflicts, fears and a desire for a "do over" now and again. The other voices in this book, from my circle of girlfriends, were also looking back and searching as I was. So "Nothin' Like I Thought" brings to you a glimpse of our life experiences, thoughts and reflections. We are black babies booming. May you find your voice among ours.

—Arlene Y. Avery Burke

Introduction—

# The Voices

*The Life & Thoughts of an Aging Baby Boomer*
*and a Few of Her Friends*

*The vignettes in this book are recollections based on real people and real events that may be enhanced for entertainment purposes. The names used for most characters have been changed to protect privacy. Whereas my girlfriends and I share what we remember and our perspective of the truth, there are some places, incidents and even persons in these vignettes that are fictional.*

*Arlene*—As the author of this book, I am a "fifty something", career woman, married thirty seven years, mother of two, who basically played by the rules, and discovered that as life goes on things rarely go along with "the plan".

*Sandra*—I am a retired, sexy sixty, divorced mother of two. My first major purchase, as an individual adult, was an automobile. I wanted a personalized license plate that represented me. After much thought, I settled on "FELINE", which represented both my appearance and stages of life. I'm now into my fifth or sixth life hoping for a total of at least nine.

*Cynthia*—I'm a married, middle aged, mother of two children, corporate executive-turned entrepreneur, with latent creative talents just beginning to be explored and tapped. I'm over one hill and searching for another.

*Susan*—I started life as a lonely, only child in search of a family. Things have changed. I'm hard to keep up with, as I stay on the move. I talk fast, think fast and drive fast. I got a late start, but I'm a quick study. A single mother of two adult children, I'm fine, forty-nine and fabulous. All I need is me.

*Elaine*—I'm a former teacher (now self employed), just turned fifty, divorced, mother of one; and, if I'd known how good it would actually feel, I would have done it years ago.

*Mavis*—I was content with my identity being my husband's identity. When he left me, I found myself. And I like what I found. I'm in a good place. I'm sharp, seventy and a sassy retiree.

*Linda*—I was almost a divorced mother of two. I'm learning to love exercise as a part of my life style. After years of up and down diet success and failure, I've learned that what goes in must be "worked" off. At this rate, I will never be unemployed.

*Carla*—I'm a retired elementary school teacher, divorced, mother of three. I believe there is a place for everything and everything should be in its place. That worked fairly well for me at work, but not at home.

*Annie*—I'm originally from a very small, rural town. Moving to a more urban environment was a life and attitude-changing event for me. I'm lovin' it. I've been teaching for thirty years and in the process of reinventing myself. I'm a divorced mother of one.

*Denise*—I'm fifty-nine and counting. I know enough and have seen or heard enough to avoid some of the pitfalls of others in this book. So I think! I'm in public relations, married and the mother of two.

*Maryann*—They call me the silver fox. When I grew up we played till the street lights came on and no one was worried. When we were thirsty, we drank from the water hose, not a bottle. Our neighbor could discipline us and not fear being shot. I learned the hard way to be a good wife and mother. A grandmother at fifty-seven, I still look forty. I'm old school. I know it and I love it.

# Chapter One
# Growing Up—My World

*Growing Up Is So Different From Being Grown Up*

# Arlene

## Shake, Rattle and Role

We grew up in the 1950s and 60s with the sound of Motown, Philadelphia and hometown Chicago Recording labels. We listened to music on 45 RPM records that made you feel good while listening to it, like: "My Girl" and "Just My Imagination" by the Temptations, "RESPECT" by Aretha Franklin, and "Have You Seen Her" by the Chi-Lites. Even today, I can't stop the smile from spreading across my face when an oldie but goodie is played on the radio.

I remember when you could buy a four inch high, Dari Delight ice cream cone for a dime and McDonalds French fries for a nickel. When my mother took us to the bank and the post office, it was a field trip. Neither place of business was located in the immediate neighborhood. We dressed up to look our best and drove to the hallowed halls. The post office and the bank were always very quiet places and once we entered, we were not allowed to be noisy.

In fact, the only thing we could hear was our footsteps echoing as we walked toward the service window; staring at the very high ceilings and the ancient paintings on the walls. Quietly whispering employees, almost hidden behind iron barred or glass windows, were busy helping customers. We stood in line for what seemed like an endless amount of time.

My parents taught us well: right from wrong, represent your family name with your best, and to work hard. These words still echo in the back of my mind. Education is critical to success. Take care of your family. Be kind. Share what you have. Give back to the community. Be good! Say grace before eating; your prayers at night. Respect your elders. You are just as good as anybody else.

Going to parties on Friday and Saturday night makes you "common". Treat others the way you expect to be treated. These were a few of the "golden rules". The fifties and sixties were a time when the real—so called—family values were gospel.

I attended what were considered "good" schools; studied hard; made excellent grades; sought advice from; and listened to the community elders. There were lots of them: other parents, relatives, neighbors, scout leaders, Sunday school teachers, Jack & Jill moms and dads, and other respected members of the community.

The list was endless. Essentially everyone was a trusted "parent" or could at least take on that role as needed. They were ordinary people with extraordinary gifts that were given freely to us kids. Long before it was popularized today, *our* community, in Evanston, Illinois, embraced the "it takes a village" concept very seriously.

Neighbors rarely moved away. Housing became available if folks died, and for the most part, homes remained in the same family for generations. Everyone knew everyone else; even the Fuller Brush man who came to the door every so often to sell his variety of brushes. It was not like today where corporate jobs require families to move every two or three years and the kids end up attending numerous elementary schools during their childhood.

Grandparents, aunts, uncles and cousins all lived close by. There were holiday, summer and special occasion gatherings on a regular basis. In my world, even divorce seemed rare. Adult affairs, for the most part, went unrecognized by us. Gossip was rare. I rarely heard any. We didn't need it, since everyone we played with was from a well-known family. If they weren't perfect, they were at least OK.

OK with our parents, the final judge of all that was good and proper. My cousin, Cheryl and I were among a rare breed in our community. Black folks with freckles! People used to look at us and wonder, "How'd that happen?" My hair was brown. Hers was long and "Howdy Doody" red, particularly unusual. Cheryl never wore a shirt on her head, pretending the sleeves were long pigtails. She had the real thing.

There were other family members with freckles too, usually a few sprinkled across the nose or a couple here and there on a cheek. The exception was my uncle Cloese (pronounced Clueeze) who lived in Georgia. Every inch of his body was dotted with freckles. This phenomenon I observed from photos, as I never did meet him personally. I guess I learned early that being different is OK. That was an important lesson for me to learn before reaching my adolescent years.

My childhood memories of growing up convey smiles, happiness and feelings of nostalgia. We laughed, we played hide and seek, and enjoyed life; shielded from and oblivious to the ills of the world that surrounded us.

## Everyday People

As a child, my world seemed perfect, fairly simple, not over indulged. Though our family didn't have a lot of money, I don't remember anyone complaining. We had everything we needed. At times, my father held three jobs to provide us with a middle class life style, though at the time the term "middle class" held no particular meaning for me. Fathers with multiple jobs did not seem odd to us, as most of our friends' fathers had more than one job too. Today this is referred to as multiple revenue streams. Everyone needs them. We had a neat three bedroom, brick home; nice clothes—some new, some home made, some hand-me-down. We always looked good!

*It's better to give than receive*, we had always heard from parents and others. Christmas brought us some things we wanted and some things we needed. We received some toys and things on our list to Santa, but he always brought underwear, gym shoes, hats and warm gloves too! A replenishing of the stuff we had outgrown. My parents and the parents of most of my best friends weren't doctors, lawyers or what many considered professionals, but they were successful in what was really important; that being setting the proper value system for us.

Though most of the African American population was located on the west side, Evanston represented a racially diverse, midsize suburban town. The west side of Evanston was mainly composed of three-bedroom brick or wood framed, two-story homes with detached garages. The yards were well maintained and homes neatly kept. There was minimal integration of the elementary schools due to these existing housing patterns.

I expected this would improve with time. I remember Foster School, my elementary school, as all black, except for the principal and some of the teachers. Foster School was where most of the black students living on the west side of Evanston attended, until it burned down. There were a few children whose parents could afford to send them to private or catholic schools as an option, but as it turned out, they didn't fare better than those of us who attended Foster School.

I walked nine blocks to and from school twice a day (we went home for lunch) until they opened a small lunchroom in the basement. The African American teachers at Foster were excellent and worked hard to encourage us to achieve and be successful citizens. Good, however, was never good enough. We had to be better. We had to be outstanding. To be noticed as "good" was not an expectation of black children, so it generally went unrecognized as a behavioral characteristic. The majority of white teachers assigned to majority black student classrooms went through the motion of teaching with little enthusiasm, excitement, encouragement or creativity. Our black teachers had to fill that gap and teach us how to be noticed in a positive light.

My mother used to host a luncheon for our teachers every June, at the end of the school year, until we graduated to junior high. I don't know of any other mother who did that. The dining table was covered with a lovely tablecloth and set with the good dishes, silver and fresh flowers. Even at a young age, I could recognize that look of surprising delight from my teachers, many of whom were white, as they entered our very neat and clean home. I didn't know enough to be insulted by it. We always had a delicious meal and polite conversation mostly about how well we kids had done that school year. I think she did this as a reminder that these were good children from a good home.

My world was steeped in middle class social values. Our parents attended many formal dances sponsored by local organizations like the Chessmen, North Shore Twelve, Bachelor and Benedict. Mother made all of her formal dresses, probably out of necessity, and they were beautiful, never having that "home made" look. During 7th grade, my sister and I took sewing classes as our initiation to this skill that we would use for a lifetime.

Our first project was an apron. A simple square, with very even seams! The teacher made a big deal out of the project that to me an idiot could have accomplished. I wouldn't have guessed that this very simple skill would be put to use making the window treatments for my first home. During 8th grade sewing class we learned to make a skirt, which was pretty much a rectangle with a waistband. We continued to hone our skills by helping our mother make our Easter outfits, homecoming and prom dresses. "Cut evenly along the edge of the pattern," she would say and "Always press the seams open and flat." This would give the finished product that "store bought" look. My pride and joy was the white brocade dress I wore as I was presented at the North Shore Twelve Cotillion in June of 1964. What we couldn't always afford to buy, we could afford to make. It was the way things were.

## To Dance With My Father Again...

As I have said, my father worked two jobs, sometimes three to keep us financially secure. His primary job was with the state highway department, where after several years, the management team recognized his abilities and eventually offered him a supervisory position. This opportunity provided a challenge for my father, as several white male employees resented taking direction from him. It took patience and some time before the men came to honor and respect him as a person and professionally. Some relationships evolved into lasting friendships until he passed away years later.

Typically, my father's day started at 4:00 a.m. at City News, where he supervised young boys on paper routes. To this day, half the guys we grew up with give credit to my father for teaching them a work ethic and keeping them on the right path. Saying half the guys is probably an exaggeration, but this is my book and my story. I know there were many young men who benefited from his advice and counsel.

It was also through this job that my father learned every household in the city of Evanston. He knew every nook, cranny and "hole" as he would call it, in town. The fact that he possessed such knowledge bore a great influence on where my sister and I were allowed to visit or attend parties.

Nothing got past him! All we had to do was give him the address and he knew exactly where the house was, who lived there and what kind of "activity" took place there. My mother deferred to him for all go/no go decisions on party invitations. There were whole streets and families that were off limits to us. Sometimes it was a blessing, getting us out of adolescent pressure situations for which we had no face-saving escape.

Daddy's evening job, two to three times a week, was cleaning up a beauty shop in Skokie, a mostly Jewish neighborhood. This is how we learned that white women were getting their hair relaxed long before black women were. The process was done behind closed curtains. Why the secret? This was information we could have all used. At any rate, this part-time job must have been for emergencies, or special needs only, as it never lasted long.

Barely reaching the age of seventy-six, our father died first. We never expected him to die so young. He had always seemed so strong and invincible. As the man of the house, he never let his ego or "manliness" get in the way of helping my mother or doing his share of household chores. There was always a rag hanging from his back pocket. He would pull it out whenever something needed dusting or just to clean up an observed mess. Frequently, he had a handful of something he'd just picked up, pulled out or cleaned off.

This man, the eldest of eight children, had helped to raise his younger brothers and sisters; no easy task. When my parents married, my mother was afraid he wouldn't want his own children as a result. She thought he might be burned out. Fortunately, he did want children. "These are mine" he said, "big difference."

When my father died, we forgot to mention in his obituary what he did for a living. I guess work or a "title" never did define who he was to us; who he was to his community. He was only five foot seven, but stood so much taller than his physical height. He was a leader in many organizations including: most worshipful master and the grand potentate of his Masons' chapter.

## Quiet Storm

My mother's first job, after we were all in school full-time, was stocking merchandise in the back of the Fair department store. The name, Fair, was actually an oxymoron. When my mother applied for the job, the store manager said, "Now Beulah, you know colored people don't work out front."

Colored people, as we were called in the fifties, weren't supposed to interact with the customers. Were they afraid if we touched them, the color would rub off? What about all those mammy nannies who nursed white children? There are so many inconsistencies in the practice of racism.

My mother, who was articulate and intelligent, with three years of college education, was relegated to folding clothes in a back room!

In the fifties, just getting the job at a big department store was seen as progress. "We should be thankful," she said. The humiliation my parents must have suffered again and again, I can only imagine, though I never really heard either of them complain.

These stories would be the material of Thanksgiving dinners in the future. My mother would go on to accomplish many "firsts". She was first to be hired at the Girl Scout head quarters; first to be hired as a school secretary in a predominantly white neighborhood; and, first to be hired in the administrative office of Evanston Public Schools as secretary to the personnel director, as well.

When she retired she was the secretary to the Superintendent. I clearly understood that it was important to finish college, so that I would have more options and not be treated like an idiot. Though I have also learned there is no guarantee of that.

## As We Stroll Along Together

The population of Evanston in the sixties was about 79,000, not much different from today. The city is land-locked with little opportunity for growth. As children, our immediate community was more like a six-block square. This is where we jumped rope after dinner; played kick ball in the alley; sang Motown songs with fake microphones; rode our bikes; played marathon-long Monopoly games; and shared peanut butter and jelly sandwiches for lunch at our impromptu back yard picnics.

Kool-aid was the beverage of choice in summer. Pop was too expensive except as an adult beverage. My mother's favorite was RC Cola. She could make a twelve-ounce bottle last all day—sometimes two. We kids could go through a gallon pitcher of Kool-aid in one sitting, which is why I guess we weren't allowed to drink the pop. The flavor was whatever you wanted it to be. It was impossible to distinguish between strawberry, raspberry or cherry flavors. Kool-aid simply came in colors, red, orange, purple or green. My brother used to experiment mixing Kool-aid with milk. He called them homemade milk shakes. Sometimes we added ice cream. His experiments only worked with the color red Kool-aid. Orange, purple or green, when mixed, were pretty much disgusting in color and taste. These drinks would turn out in various shades of gray. He never admitted how bad they were, but I caught him pouring his glass down the sink one day after telling my sister and me we should drink up or he would tell on us for wasting good food, bought with hard earned money. Of course, we weren't intimidated by this. We had a lot more to tell on him than he could ever tell on us.

Sometimes if the street was fairly clear of parked cars we could actually play kick ball with the Hendersons in the cross section of Laurel Avenue and the alley that ran parallel to the Hendersons' home. The Hendersons were a large Catholic family of ten children who could pretty much field a team with just their own brothers and sisters. Sometimes, we would split them up to even out the teams. They had skills! First and third base were the lilac bushes on opposite corners of the street and alley. Everyone had tall bushes at the end of their yards to block the view of the alley and garbage cans. Second base and home plate were old pie tins or some piece of trash we found in the alley. Often times, we marked home plate by scratching the street with a rock. Real chalk was hard to come by and was therefore saved for playing games like "squares" or hop scotch. We had a flagstone patio in our backyard, which easily adapted itself for hopscotch.

Lorraine and Luella Henderson were twin sisters and you could pretty much expect twin home runs whenever they came up to the plate. They were taller than the rest of us and quite good at sports. Kick ball could last for hours in good weather. If we were thirsty, we drank from the Henderson's water hose, but only while you waited your turn at bat.

Our good times could only be disrupted by Miss Brooks, who lived in the middle of the block. Miss Brooks bore no resemblance to the comedic TV version of Miss Brooks. Our Miss Brooks was old, scary, mean and not funny…the kind of "old" lady you had a hard time imagining was ever once young. She had wrinkled, fair skin and dark sunken eyes, covered by narrow wire rim glasses. Her long silver hair was pulled back into a tight bun. She lived alone, not even a dog. I don't think she ever married nor had children.

Her house, surrounded by a white picket fence, looked dark and deserted most of the time. This would leave you with the impression that no one was home, and no one ever saw her come or go either. Even her yard, which was home to several large trees, was dark in daylight. The fence was an easy jump if you didn't get caught.

She had an apple tree, which was tempting on cool October days. There were apples lying all over the ground and she never even offered to share. How could one old lady eat all those apples? "Get out of my yard", she would yell, "before I call the police!" Every now and then we could see her staring from a second floor window as if on watch.

These were days we stuck close to our own backyards to play. We had one golden rule when playing kickball other than the usual three outs—change sides. Everyone who dared to play understood that if you kicked the ball in Miss Brooks' yard, it was an automatic out and YOU had to go get the ball. Other than that, quitting time was when the streetlights came on.

## That's What Friends Are For

In my independent world of six blocks lived my four best girl-friends. There was rarely a time, it seemed, when all five of us were free to hang out together. One had younger brothers and sisters that needed looking after; one was an only child who could only come out to play at assigned times. I never quite knew what that schedule was. I only knew that every now and then she would show up at my back fence with a note pinned to her clothes with the length of time she could play and when she must return home.

To some extent, this annoyed my mother, whom I believe thought her mother was being selective with the time and place her child could associate with the "riffraff". I was just glad to see her. The third was also an only child, Marie, who had the best of everything. She had the best bike in the neighborhood, pretty clothes, lots of toys and stuffed animals. Her bedroom, complete with a large bed covered with a fluffy, delicate comforter and ruffled throw pillows, was full of them.

She also went to the beauty shop on a regular basis to get her hair styled. Most of us did our own hair, which amounted to a double shampoo and lots of tiny braids until it dried. Then it was restyled into a ponytail or three braids; two in the back and one on the side with colorful barrettes or ribbons at the ends. Marie always had a style with real curls made by a curling iron. She looked like Easter Sunday everyday.

Marie lived with her mother and grandparents. On the occasions we visited at her home, it was always too quiet for serious child's play. Her grandparents were nice, but didn't understand the need for little girls to make plenty of noise. So we spent a lot of time when she wasn't elsewhere or shopping, riding our bikes on the sidewalks of our neighborhood.

My first big two-wheeler bike was truly distinctive. It was purchased used, at the police auction that was held once each year. That's where one could buy, inexpensively, any unclaimed bike that had been lost or stolen. Surely someone just threw this one away. It couldn't have been stolen! It wasn't worth the risk. Boy, that thing was ugly – a forest green frame with dull, not shiny, *hand painted*, silver handlebars! The chrome had long worn away so the hand painting had that ripple effect of brush strokes, which poorly covered up the chipped and cracked old chrome beneath. The bike had no brand name. It had no fenders. You may say "so what, racers don't have fenders." But this was no racer. It had only one speed, my speed. And fenders can be real important when it rains. Get the picture? If I didn't beat the rainstorm home, my back was as freckled as my face. I didn't like that bike, but it provided good transportation. It was faster than two feet walking.

We would travel west on Emerson, a well traveled street by car, to Leland, quiet and residential; then left for two blocks, back east on Church, another busy street where the high school was located; and then back up Hartrey with a slight jog to Laurel, where my cousin and Denise lived; and then back to Emerson where Annie, Marie and I lived. This was our signature route. On this ride we could pick up almost everyone and then retrace the ride over and over. Now and then we ventured to an unknown, less traveled street just as an adventure.

The last girlfriend in my geographically defined world was my cousin, Cheryl, who was more like a sister, since we were only two months apart in age. So we grew up and experienced a lot of life together. If she wasn't at my house, I was at hers. We played every board game known to man, Monopoly, Chutes and Ladders, Candyland, Chinese checkers, Checkers, Scrabble, Clue, Sorry and other games that required expert eye-hand coordination like jacks, paddle ball and pick up sticks.

We baked cakes, rode bikes, jumped double Dutch, taught each other dances, shared secrets, dreamed with the J.C. Penny and Sears catalogs; held picnics in the back yard, took piano lessons together, attended the same church, went to the movies, the beach, the parties; everything together. We never did any activity to the purposeful exclusion of the other. The only times we were separated was when it was time for her to visit relatives in Indiana or me in Wisconsin. We even attended the same college for two years post high school graduation.

## Easy Like Sunday Morning

The very first church my brother, sister and I attended was New Hope CME. It was walking distance from home. This was key as we were required to attend Sunday school every Sunday whether our parents went or not. Daddy was a member of Mt. Zion Baptist and Mom, Ebenezer AME. Both churches were reachable only by car.

New Hope was a very small, intimate congregation with dedicated Sunday school teachers. Off we went each Sunday; my brother in a suit and my sister and I donned in our frilly dresses and patent leather shoes, gleaming with a fresh application of Vaseline petroleum jelly. Our purses swung from side to side as we skipped merrily along the sidewalk.

Inside, safely held in the zipper section, was one dime for the offering, a tissue, and maybe a stick of gum for chewing after church. We sang in the youth choir and led the service during big church once a month. It's what every well-brought-up, middle-class child did in our neighborhood.

Classes were held in every nook and cranny of the church. My class, taught by Ms. Pringle, was held in a closet. I swear to this day I don't know how they were able to fit so many chairs in that tiny little room. One advantage of the closet was that it was quiet. We didn't hear the other children reading their lessons, answering questions or reciting their bible verses.

In summer, we were quite happy to reach the end of our class and to escape to fresh air and more freedom of movement. Once we had dropped our dime in the offering basket and said the final prayer, we were off to wherever. Ms. Pringle made us take turns saying the prayer. I said mine so softly that hardly anyone could hear me. Sometimes we stayed for big church, where the adults worshipped, or sometimes we just headed home. If we stayed, we sat in the middle of the pews and never the aisle seat.

That seat proved dangerous whenever old folks got "happy" during the service. Sometimes they danced up and down the aisles shouting in tongues and reaching out for whomever they could reach. Whoever they touched sometimes got the Holy Ghost next and started jumping and shouting too.

Whatever was happening to them was frightening to me, so the middle child sat in the middle seat on Sundays. As we got a little older we ventured further to attend Bethel AME church, a longer walk located east of Dodge Avenue. Crossing Dodge was a big deal. It was like a neighborhood dividing line venturing into another part of town.

It was my job to start dinner, or that part of the meal that mom had left instructions for me to do. Usually that amounted to turning on the oven, which already held a seasoned pot roast, and making scalloped potatoes, my specialty. By the time mom returned from church, the aroma from the kitchen oven was in full force. She finished the meat and vegetables and we would have dinner early, around three o'clock.

Most times Sunday ended with a family drive north on beautiful tree-lined Sheridan Road, with its long driveways leading to huge set back old mansions. We imagined what it would be like to live in one of those turn-of-the-century homes, with back yards overlooking Lake Michigan. The ride was never complete without a stop at Homers Ice Cream Shop for homemade ice cream cones— two dips, peach and chocolate chip.

## Nothin' Like the Real Thing

We grew up in a time where you had the good stuff and the every day stuff. In the living room was good stuff, so you didn't eat or play in there, not even watch TV. It would ruin the sofa. The TV was in the family room. The dining room had good stuff too, so we only ate in there when we had company or on Sundays and holidays.

There were good dishes, the china and silver, and the everyday stuff. The every day dishes were plastic, melamine or inexpensive place settings purchased with S&H green stamps. S&H green stamps were disbursed at department stores, gas stations and other places, based on the amount of your original purchase. It could sometimes take weeks to fill the pages of those books, but once you had several filled, you could use them like money to buy every day household items like dishes and folding chairs.

Most people's everyday glasses were not made of glass. They were plastic or Tupperware and therefore unbreakable. The every day glasses that could break were "ex" mason jars or jelly jars which were of no consequence, if broken. Jelly jars were especially usable as juice glasses as they were usually very small. Glassware for every day use was where my family differed from most. We drank from monogrammed glasses every meal, every day.

My friends were impressed. Our glasses were of fine glass, in all sizes, made with beautifully etched designs like roses and letters on them. Before you assume that my parents spent money frivolously on such an extravagance, here's the real deal. My sister's godmother, Aunt Gerry, worked at a glass factory. Any time mistakes were made in monogramming the glasses, she got to bring them home, so we had an endless supply of GVB or JMA or cWc juice, water, highball and wine glasses. I guess they made a lot of mistakes at that factory. It was cool.

## I've Got So Much Honey, the Bees Envy Me

I think I inherited my love of gardening from my father. Daddy's yard was always the unstated pride of the neighborhood. At the front door were evergreen bushes and a purple plum tree that bore tiny pink flowers every spring. The lawn was green and impeccable, never a dandelion in sight. That's because on his way inside each evening from work, daddy would take a jackknife from his back pants pocket and dig up any weed that dared to poke its head above ground. There was no homeland security, so most men carried pocketknives attached to key chains on a regular basis for perfunctory uses.

We had white—with a slight hint of purple—morning glories growing up and along the fence, which separated our back yard from the neighbor's concrete driveway. At the back of the yard were thick lilac and snowball bushes, fragrant in the spring, serving the dual purpose of blocking the alley and its unsightly garbage cans.

His pride and joy was the rock garden, centered with a trellis of climbing rose bushes of all colors, peach, red and yellow. There were snapdragons, rose moss and hostas, planted between various rock formations. Colorful flowers of all kinds and sizes, surrounded our house, serving as a private enclosure from the outside world. In this beautiful garden would be held my wedding reception, years later, on a warm and sunny August Saturday afternoon.

My own garden, over the years, has become the grateful recipient of many of his cuttings from peonies, hostas and lilies. It's a way I keep a little piece of him with me always. On one occasion, I casually mentioned how much I liked the purple plum at the front door and would miss it once my parents moved into their new home in another town.

A few days later, there it was at my front door. He had dug it up for me. No doubt my daddy would have given me the world if he could.

## It Feels Like Home to Me

My paternal grandparents' names were William and Mary Elizabeth (Dent) Avery. My grandmother was an excellent cook and house-keeper, a product of her southern upbringing, no doubt. Her large kitchen was devoid of measuring utensils of any kind. The preferred instrument of measurement was her hands; a palm, a pinch or a finger full of whatever ingredient was all that was needed.

When we visited, there was something good warming on the stove and a pitcher of fresh lemonade in the refrigerator. My grandmother did not believe in artificial ingredients. She purchased the best of everything for her recipes. Good smells emanated from her kitchen with just a hint of bleach. That was because she washed everything in bleach: the dishes, the linoleum floor, the counters and tabletops.

Her floor was mopped and scrubbed daily. "Too many people live here", she would say, not to maintain a spotless, and germ free environment. And the only way to kill germs, to her way of thinking, was bleach.

Grandma was a large woman. So as she aged, she had to use two canes to maintain balance and get around. Without her canes, she would lean on furniture with each step taken, sometimes resting a minute on the arm of a chair or the sofa. This took a great deal of effort, so our main task during visits was to fetch things for her.

If there were several cousins visiting at the same time, she would confuse us, calling out a litany of names before getting to the correct one. "Come here Joey, Ricky, Billy, uh Mike, uh Jimmy, boy you know who I'm talking to." "Get over here!" We would stand there staring and laughing until she got it right. Sometimes you had to duck her cane for doing that.

Her favorite place was the front porch. With a shawl wrapped around her shoulders, she could sit and rock for hours. Everyone in the neighborhood knew her and spoke while passing. "Morning Ms. Avery, nice day Ms. Avery, how are you today?"

Sitting on Grandma's porch is where I learned to love country music. She sat in her rocker and I sat on the concrete ledge with my feet dangling over the side. We would sit listening to her transistor radio, which always tuned to WMAQ Country Radio. She remembered herself the young girl back in Appling, Georgia, while I only imagined what it was like. The first time I actually traveled to Georgia would be as an adult moving with my husband to Atlanta as a result of his job transfer.

It was nothing like I imagined or feared. I expected the KKK in every neighborhood just waiting for us to make a wrong move. What I found, at least in my Cobb County sub division, were friendly people who liked to do the same things I did; play tennis, cook gourmet meals, read and play cards. Our neighbors were visiting with us on our first day, before the moving van was empty of our belongings, bringing sweet potato pies and chocolate chip cookies.

Grandma Avery was an in charge kind of person. She knew what she wanted and usually got just that. As the mother of eight children, discipline was central to order. If you misbehaved, she would have you select your own switch from the tree and bring it to her. Fortunately, I never had to make that trip. I watched my cousins plenty of times. They never learned that grandma didn't play.

Even her own children, as adults, were afraid to smoke cigarettes or drink alcohol in front of her. My dad was the only one who smoked cigars in front of her, and she never said a word. Maybe because he was the oldest, he enjoyed more latitude. The others, all of whom smoked cigarettes, never dared to try. Granddad Avery used to smoke a pipe, even though it was rarely lit while we were there. We could, nevertheless, smell the sweet aroma throughout the house.

Unlike Grandma, he was a small, quiet and gentle man. We could do most anything with him and never hear a complaint. He spent a lot of time in the living room watching the Chicago Cubs or upstairs in his bedroom sitting in what appeared to be quiet reflection. It might have been his way of escaping us. When he did speak, you did whatever he said just out of sheer surprise. The only times he really showed excitement was while watching the Cubs play baseball. You could tell he was excited by how fast his foot would shake up and down as he sat cross-legged in a hardback chair.

Sometimes Grandma would steal his remote control and hit the button just as the Cubs got a hit or scored a run. He never seemed angry. He just said, "Go get the clicker from your grandma's pocket." He left us the same way he lived, quietly rocking in his chair, pipe in hand, alone in the bedroom. As he took his last breath, he asked one of my cousins to, "Go get your grandma and tell her I'm dying." And then he was gone. Before I really had a chance to know my granddad Avery well, who he was and the life he had traveled through, he was gone.

## Got To Be There

I remember the loud tick-tock of the ebony clock on the buffet of my Aunt Carrie and Uncle John Fleming's house. It was a sound of calm assurance that made you feel relaxed and safe. Aunt Carrie was my paternal grandmother's sister. They lived one block from each other in Evanston. Spending the night with them was like a visit to the set of Bonanza except it was a very quiet house.

There were no children. In the bedroom where we slept were twin beds with end tables on each side. On top were lantern-shaped lamps that would remind you of old kerosene lit lamps. We pretended to blow them out before we went to sleep. A tall, mirrored, mahogany dresser, with lace doilies placed neatly on top of each side drawer, and one in the middle, was the first piece of furniture you saw upon entering the room.

It was the most beautiful dresser I had ever seen, very old and elegant like the Queen of England must have owned. On one lace doily laid a silver comb, brush and mirror set that no one dared to use. I think it was a static display for show.

Their house exhibited dozens of old pictures of distinguished looking elderly people on every wall and every available flat surface. Most were of deceased relatives. There was an antique brocade sofa and three chairs protected with plastic covers. Beside each was an end table holding a lamp and crystal candy dish. Uncle John smoked cigars, so there was usually a stinky half-smoked butt left in an ashtray.

In the dining room was a huge sculpted, beveled mirror over the buffet, filled with fine china and stemware. Occupying the middle of the room was a dark cherry wood dining table, large enough to seat eight or ten people. This was a house filled with expensive and fragile items you didn't find in a house where children live.

I don't know if Aunt Carrie and Uncle John ever wanted children. I once over heard Aunt Carrie say her sister Mary, my grandmother, had enough for the both of them. They only lived a block a part;

however I don't recall them visiting each other much. Being open seven days a week, their grocery store pretty much consumed their lives.

On some occasions when my parents attended formal dances, which would result in very late evenings out, my sister and I would spend the night with Aunt Carrie and Uncle John. We would sit at the dining table and play paper dolls or sometimes watch Rocky and Bullwinkle cartoons on the only TV set in the house, which was located in their bedroom.

They had a bed that sat very high off the floor. We weren't supposed to sit on it, and with just one chair available, sitting on the floor made trying to see over it difficult. We mostly amused ourselves in other ways. Sometimes we would go and help in the store. I used to love to watch Uncle John grind the big chunks of beef into long streams of red meat trailing down to the butcher-block table. Sometimes he would let me turn the grinder.

The next morning, Aunt Carrie would commence to preparing breakfast for us: scrambled eggs, grits, pork chops, cereal, toast, biscuits, fruit, bacon, milk and juice would be on the table. Not having children, I guess, made it difficult to know what and how much they consume in one meal. Trying to be polite, my sister and I did the best we could to eat as much as possible. We stuffed ourselves! It never failed; Aunt Carrie would give the same report when mom asked how things went. "Well they were good girls, but they don't eat much!"

## Stone Soul Picnic

Aunt Carrie and Uncle John's home occupied a large lot in Evanston, which also housed Fleming's Grocery Store and a detached garage. Inside the garage was Uncle John's mint condition, shiny, black Oldsmobile. It emerged every so often to be washed and waxed whether it was needed or not. I never saw him drive it anywhere.

Between their home and the store was a large yard perfect for our family picnics during the summer. All my aunts, uncles and cousins on my father's side of the family would gather and consume large amounts of food. It was convenient having a grocery store in the family. If we ran out of anything, Uncle John would open up the store and get whatever we needed. For us that meant, candy and ice cream!

After eating, we sat around and listened to music and stories about the old days, people and family in Georgia. Aunt Carrie used to tell us of old beaus that Big Daddy, my great grandfather, didn't approve of and the times she used to get in trouble at school. I liked those stories best. Now and then she would tell stories of the side of the family that was "passing".

Everybody had folks in their family light enough to pass for white. Life was easier for them if they did, so we didn't blame them for making that decision. We used to joke about white folks today who might be "related" and don't even know it. We know them when we see them as we look for signs of familiarity. They are the folks with slightly thicker lips, maybe thicker; wavy hair, even if it is blond, and a little more melanin in their skin tone.

Today, I long for more details of these stories of long ago. They have been lost in the impatience of a young child, more eager to play jacks and jump rope, than sit still and listen. I wish I had taken the time to record them.

At these family picnics, all of my cousins, about twenty of us, would be there. For many summers, we ate, laughed and played ball; before we all scattered—scattered to far away places, other states, islands in the sun; scattered to our own homes, newly started families, the military, college, the streets; and jail. We were the same then, in each other's eyes.

## People Get Ready

For a time, my father worked in—and then purchased—Fleming's Grocery Store from Aunt Carrie and Uncle John, who decided to retire to Arizona. We have a second home there today. Who knew that would happen? At the store, daddy did most of the butchering. Like Uncle John, he would wrap the meat in large sheets of white paper, weigh it and tie it with a string before finally writing the price on the package. I think he really enjoyed operating the store.

Unfortunately, retirement for the Fleming's didn't last long. My daddy had to find another way to support his growing family. Before he knew it, Aunt Carrie and Uncle John were back from Arizona. They hated every minute of retirement in hot and dusty Arizona. They acquired the store back from my father and continued to work until Uncle John died some years later. My father tried opening his own grocery in another neighborhood, but the store was small and the foot traffic was light, so once again he moved on to another vocation.

Fleming's Grocery Store was located only a block from Foster Elementary School. Most times, if we took the long way home, we would pass by and Aunt Carrie would give us a Popsicle to split or a piece of candy. We thought they were rich and I guess they were. They were the first in the family to die and leave an inheritance to almost all of us.

## Welcome Home

Every other summer, we traveled to Pueblo, Colorado to visit our maternal grandparents, Oscar and Beulah Phillips Baker. They were a rather unusual looking couple when together. Grandma had a large frame, nearly six feet tall, while Granddad maybe topped five feet-four and was bald. I always wondered, but never asked, how they got together.

Grandma Baker had three sisters, Irene, Vivian and Ruth, who, when they lined up for pictures, looked like a descending ski slope; from Beulah P., as they called her, at nearly six feet, to Aunt Ruth, just barely five feet tall. They always posed sideways, shoulders slightly forward, skirts and knees slightly lifted upward. They reminded me of one-time showgirls, now grown old.

We also visited with our cousins Mickey and Coralie, whose father was my mother's brother, Uncle Randall. The trip would take two days, whether by car or train. If daddy couldn't make the trip with us, we would take the California Zephyr, a soaring, silver engine train. Colorado afforded an opportunity to visit—for real—our TV imagined wild, wild West; but except for the mountains, it felt less like being on the set of Bonanza, than Aunt Carrie and Uncle John's house.

Our grandparents' home had the look and feel of any standard grandma's house: homemade quilts on the beds; a screen door that slammed and bounced as we ran outside; old pictures of relatives hanging on the walls; plastic covered furniture with doilies on the arms; a rocking chair in the corner; and the smell of cookies baking in the kitchen.

Pueblo, Colorado, where they lived, was a small town of mostly Mexicans, Indians, whites and just a handful of African Americans. I used to think that most of the black folks in town had to be related to me somehow. Though Pueblo seemed small, everything else appeared expansive compared to home. The sky was big, painted with majestic mountains; some snow capped and others bright orange. There were tall trees and land as far as you could see.

Granddad Baker, unexpectedly, was more like a farmer than a cowboy. He dressed in blue jean coveralls every day. In the back yard, where we played most of the time, was an old goat or two and his prize possessions, the gaming cocks. Now to us, they looked like chickens, but to Granddad they were fighting cocks. They strutted around the yard as if they owned the place.

We weren't supposed to play with them, but my brother did all the time. One time he nearly strangled one to death by carrying it by its neck into the house to show my mother how pretty it was. "Look what I found mom," he said with a snaggle-toothed grin, as every adult in the house jumped out of their chairs and ran to the chicken's rescue. He never quite knew what he had done wrong, and it sure caused a commotion.

Across the street from my grandparents' home was a large cemetery. My grand parents, as well as great grandparents, are buried there. On the opposite side of the cemetery lived our cousins, Mickey and Coralie. We could either walk around the cemetery, about three blocks, or cut through as a short cut to their house. If we stopped to examine the headstones, it was like reading the family history.

Mickey and Coralie were near our same age, so we enjoyed playing together almost every day. Coralie was cursed with a very fair complexion, so Aunt Gladys didn't let her play outside in the sun much, which limited our activities on some days. We thought that was mean of Aunt Gladys. Not understanding her reasons, we just moaned and let it go.

Sometimes, cousins Morty, Diane, Reggie and Kenneth would join us and we played all day; completely forgetting about the time. One day, as the sun was setting, we knew we'd better hustle home for dinner. So we decided to cut through the cemetery instead of walking around.

The walk, at dusk, didn't feel the same. It was no longer the town cemetery; it became the graveyard; the graveyard from every scary movie we'd ever seen. My brother started to make haunting noises and ran off ahead of us, laughing as he went. If we had continued to walk, everything would have been normal, but when he ran, we started to run.

We could hear our footsteps echoing among the tombstones. It sounded like people (ghosts) were chasing us. My heart was pounding. Grandma's house never seemed so far away and my brother had vanished. We made a wrong turn and soon lost our way. "Where's the gate?" Tears were streaming down our faces. We knew we were going to die that night in the graveyard. As the trees cast dark shadows, they seemed to move with us at every step.

Just as we were circling in panic, he appeared again from nowhere and led us safely home. The minute we walked in the door mama could see on our faces that something was amiss. She asked, "What's wrong?" We answered in triplicate: "Nothin'."

## Strawberry Fields

Memories of growing up are split between home with our parents, and summers with Aunt Erma and Uncle Leonard Jenkins in Madison, Wisconsin. This was before cheeseheads were called cheeseheads. Aunt Erma was my mother's older sister. My brother, sister and I have rich memories of the simplest things during those summer vacations: picking raspberries; going fishing with Uncle Leonard, root beer floats; watching dairy cows being milked; meetings of the Women's Society of Christian Service; mud pies; day camp; tea parties; and playing paper dolls for hours and hours and hours. With as many outfits as my sister and I made for these dolls, it's a wonder neither of us grew up to be dress designers.

Aunt Erma taught us many of the practical and creative things of life: being well-behaved; sharing; acceptance of people who are different from ourselves; gardening; weaving; embroidering; and making our own copper enameled jewelry. She owned a huge wooden weaving loom where we spent at least some time each day adding to the latest rug, place mat or gift item, to be shared at the Women's Society.

Aunt Erma persuaded us to play with the white and the black kids in the neighborhood. After all, she would say, "We need to know how to get along with everyone." At home in Illinois, our neighborhoods were not nearly as integrated as Madison, and everyone seemed to be at the same level economically. My sister and I used to host lovely "tea parties" in the backyard with the neighbors' kids invited.

These neighbors included a family of ruffians that lived up the hill—a group of "dusty" brothers (we called such because they were dusty and dirty all of the time). Their clothes were dusty, especially their shoes and socks. Their hair was dusty. Their skin was dusty. I guess they never heard of Ponds cold cream or Vaseline petroleum jelly. I don't think they bathed nor had their clothes washed often.

We never saw or met their mother and father. I guess they were allowed to play outside all day because they were always in the street throwing rocks or some other annoying thing. We tried to exclude them from our parties by not making much effort to let them know when they were being held. To be more aggressive would have disappointed Aunt Erma's "acceptance and tolerance of all" value system. Somehow, these dusty boys always knew when each event was to be held.

They showed up to eat all the cookies and always broke something. My sister and I preferred "refined guests" at our parties, but as I mentioned earlier, Aunt Erma didn't believe in exclusion. We never questioned the importance or significance of that wisdom.

## Get On the Good Foot

I remember black, white and Cuban families living in the same neighborhood. This integrated community coexisted very well in the 1950s in Madison. I guess the one thing everyone had in common was survival. No one had much money. Everyone did what was possible with what they had and was thankful for it.

This was not a time when states were referred to as "red" or "blue". It held no significance. Republicans didn't seem any better or worse than Democrats except in southern states where they were both to be feared. Fear of the "South" was something we learned early in life. We had all heard and read stories about Klan lynchings and segregation. We knew the South was not somewhere you wanted to go often or be caught out after dark.

Here, in this Madison, Wisconsin neighborhood, everyone knew each other and basically had the same goals and the same life. Parents wanted the best for their children, to live the American dream. And no one was afraid of the dark! There was only one dim streetlight at each intersection.

Aunt Erma read the Bible every morning. The day didn't start until that was done. So reading Bible stories was always part of our vacation activities, as well. This is how we kept ourselves busy while she studied. My favorite was "Daniel in the Lion's Den" and Old Testament stories about Noah, Shadrach, Meshach and Abednego.

God delivered these people from terrible circumstances. In my world the hero must always come out on top. Not realistic, I know, but it's what still makes me feel good even today. I just have to believe that eventually, that's the way things will end up. My sister is the same way. She still watches thirty-year-old Perry Mason mysteries on TV, where the bad guy always gets caught and goes to jail. Sometimes you just need simplicity.

Aunt Erma was also a member of the Women's Society of Christian Service. Once in a while, we attended meetings with her. Children were seen but not heard in my day, so we never heard what they said or saw what they did in these meetings that would seemingly last all day. Most of the members lived on farms, which afforded my sister and me the opportunity to play once again, as if we were visiting Bonanza's Ponderosa. I was really into Westerns. We pretended to be the Cartwrights' little sisters or wives, living in the days of the Wild West.

These W.S.C.S. women owned horses, cows, barns, antiques and lots of land to explore. We brushed the horses and fed the cows while awaiting the end of the meeting. I don't remember much about the Christian service they provided, but I do remember the home cooked food they prepared.

Everything was so fresh and colorful; caramel cakes, strawberry pies and chocolate chip cookies that were out of this world. Oh yea, there were fresh garden vegetables too! Most importantly, there were no restrictions. We were allowed to eat all we wanted.

We also spent a number of afternoons and evenings at Blessed Martin, a mission on the hill, at the top of Beld Street. It was about a fifteen-minute walk from the Jenkins's home. As I recall, this is where we did volunteer work for the Indians. Though, per their website today, it states that St. Martin House, as it is now called, was founded in 1946 by Bishop Jerome Hastrich for the purpose of evangelizing and serving the African-American community in Madison.

It has evolved into a Catholic community center; providing religious education and social and educational activities for children and adults. Blessed Martin/St. Martin House has been a groundbreaking effort to develop positive working relationships among people of diversity.

Madison, Wisconsin, I think, was ahead of other states in such an effort during the fifties. Included in its programs were volunteers who helped prepare and serve a free community meal, several evenings a week, for both on-site and carryout consumption. Today, in addition to these same programs, a nurse assists the guests of St. Martin House with health care concerns, and provides blood pressure and glucose checks and other services.

During the summer, a Children's Christian day camp gives neighborhood children a fun and enriching experience in a safe, values-based environment. In my childhood, values meant open minds and open hearts. It meant helping those less fortunate than yourself, sharing, being kind to everyone, even "dusty boys". It was not defined by a narrow vision of sexual orientation or who should marry whom.

## Betcha by Golly, Wow

Betcha never had a meal like Erma's trash. My Aunt Erma was a talented and creative cook. I admired her ability to make up her own recipes on the fly. She could take leftovers and make you think she had started from scratch. Sometimes when we peeked in the pots and pans before dinner, we couldn't always recognize what was for dinner.

It just wasn't your ordinary meat and potatoes kind of meal. Often there would be some kind of game, like rabbit stew. There would be skillets and pans on every eye of the stove with something bubbling inside; and, usually something baking in the oven; either home made bread or a sweet delight for dessert. We would ask her what she was preparing and she would always respond "Oh, just a little of Erma's trash." Best "trash" we ever ate!

There were lots of recipe books in her cabinets and we never saw Aunt Erma use them. I guess by then the recipes were in her head or they just came to her spiritually. She obviously knew good taste. I think Aunt Erma weighed about three hundred pounds from eating her own cooking!

## Mercy, Mercy, Mercy

One of our favorite pastimes in Wisconsin was making mud pies. Do little girls still do that? This, of course, was how I learned the joy of cooking. I imagined myself making everything my aunt did. My "trash" however, was truly trash. My sister and I made everything from cakes and cookies, to meatballs and biscuits, which we considered fairly balanced meals. We used marbles for pretend peas and buttons as other vegetables.

My brother was never quite sure where his marbles were disappearing to. He just knew he was always short a few. Aunt Erma and Uncle Leonard "ate" all of our delicious meals. I, of course, would never prepare a mud pie meal unless all the dishes, pots and pans were clean, absolutely spotless. It used to drive them nuts, that I wouldn't touch the dishes unless they were clean!

They couldn't understand the importance for me of starting with clean dishes, even if I was going to ultimately put mud in them. One thing I liked less than dusty boys was dirty dishes. After a meal preparation, I never wanted to clean the dishes either. I made them do it. The cook doesn't have to clean up. It's rule number one. And besides, they shouldn't give children dirty stuff to play with!

They used to refer to me as the pensive one. I don't think it had anything to do with the mud pies though. I'm sure they had a lot of other names for me too, like the "little dictator". Like "Little Miss I must have everything perfect". Like "Miss I only want half a hamburger, will you split it with me" and then I get hungry and eat the whole thing. Well, it was *MY* hamburger!

## Give It Up or Turn it A Loose

Uncle Leonard was an outdoorsman and a builder. He was tall and slim, despite Aunt Erma's cooking; but more probably because of his ulcers. He walked like his feet hurt all the time. Even when he was barefoot, he swayed side to side with each step. Uncle Leonard had real long toes that were permanently scrunched up to the ball of his foot, with corns atop each one. He said it was from wearing shoes that were too small as a boy in Kentucky.

His mother couldn't afford to buy him new shoes every time his feet out grew the old ones, and his feet, it seemed, wouldn't stop growing. His shoes would hurt so badly that he had to walk down the hill backwards on his way to school! His childhood taught him to live with little and I guess he learned to live with pain too.

Having little also encouraged Uncle Leonard to hone his skills and do for himself what he couldn't afford to buy or pay someone else to do. He built the house that he and Aunt Erma lived in, after work and on weekends. Thanks to Uncle Leonard, shop class, for me, was a breeze in junior high, as I had already become acquainted with the tools of the trade much earlier in my uncle's garage.

Among many delightful experiences I had with Uncle Leonard, one of the most memorable was when he taught me how to bait a fishing hook. I loved fishing, but I hated baiting the hook. You already know how I feel about dirty things. My pole was a simple bamboo stick; with a line tied at the end to a little red and white plastic bobber, attached to a hook, on the end of the fishing line. Baiting the hook was a simple skill which was emotionally difficult for me to master.

Remember the mud pie story? I knew what to do; I just didn't want to do it. One hot afternoon, Uncle Leonard refused to put the worm on my hook. It was time for me to grow up, so he said, and get over my disdain of messy, slimy things. It was also genuine fear on my part, which I refused to admit. So, while trying to hold on to that yucky, wiggly worm, I started to panic as it curled snuggly around my fingers.

It wouldn't stop moving, sliding between my fingers, scrunching up and down my hand and wrist. I tried to shake it loose, but the worm stuck like glue. As I tried frantically to shake it off of me, I screamed hysterically, "Get it off, Uncle Leonard." "Get it off of me!" The look on his face mirrored mine and clearly indicated danger ahead.

During this "growth" episode, I nearly capsized the fishing boat we were in. It rocked recklessly back and forth with the edge slightly touching the surface of the lake, spilling a little water into the bottom of the boat with each rock. This, of course, alarmed me further, and I almost knocked Uncle Leonard over board while he tried, as best he could, to calm me down.

We survived, barely. He didn't argue with me about those worms again. From then on, he patiently baited my hooks with each request from me. I still had to clean the fish that I caught when we returned home. Of course, I didn't like that either.

It was like chasing a frog, flopping all over the place, before you could finally still the creature by cutting its head off. The worst was over after that. Removing the scales was merely a messy task with scales flying everywhere, as you scraped with a special tool. My brother looked at me as if I were an idiot. Such a girl I was. To this day, I still don't order fish at a restaurant unless the head is already removed.

There's nothing like the taste of fresh water Wisconsin Blue Gill for dinner. I can still hear them sizzling in the frying pan, as the aroma of dinner traveled outside to the front steps where we sat, awaiting the call. Every day we sat waiting, counting the cars on passing freight trains. Sixty, sixty-one, sixty-two, *"Dinner's ready!"*

## Love and Happiness

Aside from baiting a hook, and before life removed the innocence, our incredibly patient Uncle Leonard provided our first lessons in democracy. Maybe his patience was derived from the fact that he and Aunt Erma didn't have any children of their own to drive them nuts on a regular basis. Anybody can be patient for two weeks during the summer, right?

Many vital decisions, during those Wisconsin summers, were made through a democratic process. We learned the importance of voting up front and personally. While traveling through the country to the many interesting places from which childhood memories are made, we would fall asleep in the back seat of the car on our way home. The excitement of the trip and activities we experienced would leave us with all energy spent.

Though we appeared to be unconscious in the back, my sister and I possessed a most unusual talent of being able to "smell" a hamburger and A&W root beer, while passing this restaurant at a speed of fifty five miles per hour along the highway. It was uncanny how we would instantly awake and ask for a cold A&W. It had to be a cold, frosted mug with one scoop of vanilla ice cream floating on top.

Aunt Erma, always on the side of good nutrition, and not spoiling our dinner, would conservatively state those concerns. Then we'd take a VOTE. Our vote (the kid vote) counted as one YES, and her vote (the adult vote) would be NO; and dear old Uncle Leonard voted with us kids at every opportunity. He broke the tie, and we not only had root beer floats, but burgers and fries also! Poor Uncle Leonard caught a lot of flack for that.

Aunt Erma could have put the "freeze" on these votes, except she never did. I think she enjoyed spoiling us as much as Uncle Leonard. Someone had to be the voice of reason, even if we elected not to listen to it. Of course, we still had to eat dinner and all our vegetables without complaint after one of these occasions. It's good to be spoiled by adoring relatives.

## Who Let the Dogs Out?

Aunt Erma and Uncle Leonard owned hunting dogs, six or so, at any given time. The breeds were either Beagle, Lab or both, depending on the year. Now, to me, my sister and brother, dogs are people too. Dogs are part of the family. They may be pets, but they live in the house with you, eat, sleep and play with you. They may even learn tricks for neighborhood demonstrations. After all, our dog back home in Illinois did. We discovered this to be not the case with hunting dogs.

Diamond and Valarie were husband and wife; mother and father to five puppies. They lived outside in fenced-in doghouses. Diamond, a large Golden Lab, lived in one pen and Valarie and the pups in the other. They lived there year round, even during the winters. They earned their keep, of course, by being good hunting dogs.

Hunting dogs are not for child's play—a concept we never quite understood. So one day we let the dogs out. We brought them inside "where they belonged"! Diamond, the male dog, proceeded to immediately mark his territory. That meant he peed on the leg of every piece of furniture in the house.

I was amazed by how big this dog's bladder must be, and evidently it was full, because as he left his *mark*; there seemed to be no shortage in supply. Boy, were we in big trouble! We also learned, as we gave chase to remove Diamond from the house, that he was really good at the game of tag. As we slipped on every throw rug in the house, we were fortunate that nothing was destroyed in the process.

Nothing was damaged, except our pride. That was the first and last time we witnessed unbridled anger in Uncle Leonard. True to his nature though, he didn't tell Aunt Erma on us. She would have punished us big time. He just made us clean every speck of pee on the floor and toppled furniture. The clean up was punishment enough. We were glad to comply, so Aunt Erma never had to know what we had done. We learned a significant lesson. There are dogs and then there are *real* dogs.

## Sisters, You Gotta Have Sisters

My mother had two older brothers who lived in Colorado and California. Aunt Erma was her only sister and nearest relative. They were different from each other, yet had a close and special relationship. Aunt Erma was plain and lived a simple, home made life. My mother had style and loved pretty things.

They were both creative and musically talented. My mother sang while my aunt played the piano. Aunt Erma was not blessed with children, which I never knew if it was by choice or a physical inability. So, my mother shared us with her sister. I think they both needed that. We called Aunt Erma and Uncle Leonard our "country parents".

The experiences we had were so different from living in the Chicago Suburbs. We went to the Wisconsin Dells to see real Indians on reservations; to visit the cave of the mounds; bird habitats; farms; and all that Wisconsin had to offer. Wisconsin was like a whole different world. Everything was alive and colorful, fresh and open. The air, the water, the foods we ate were all fresh. I could easily produce the "Explore Wisconsin" Chamber of Commerce commercials one sees on television today.

On a daily basis, we helped to plant and weed Aunt Erma's garden. It was exciting to watch the garden grow. Some days were really hot and sticky between the narrow rows of vegetables; where flies and mosquitoes sometimes ate us alive. The fruits of our labor were worth every hot, itchy moment. We grew sweet, juicy strawberries and raspberries; the best tasting green beans and potatoes ever. The corn was so sweet, it melted in your mouth and didn't need butter, salt or pepper.

We were never jealous when my brother participated in activities that were just for the "men", like hunting and baiting the hook or traps. This, I did not mind, and we all helped cook the "catch", whether it was fish or game. If it had to be skinned and cleaned before we could cook, I never volunteered for that part of the job, too messy.

My job was to keep wood in the fireplace, so it didn't go out, and kept us warm. It was also hard for me to think about the hunted animal's mother and how she must be missing her offspring. I just couldn't look into those sad eyes. Wisconsin meals meant squirrel or rabbit for breakfast instead of bacon. This I had to get used to, as initially everything seemed to remind me more of a storybook character, rather than a meat.

Instead of beef or chicken for dinner, we had pheasant, quail or venison. Pheasant wasn't bad; similar to chicken; could be tolerated. Venison, I could just never bring myself to enjoy. It was like eating "Bambi". All vegetables and fruits we enjoyed came from the garden, of course. What we didn't eat fresh, during those summers, we helped to can or freeze. Then at Thanksgiving and Christmas, we enjoyed the harvest all over again.

Thanksgiving was more than a family gathering at the Jenkins's home in Madison. There were always two or three invited guests; foreign students from the University of Wisconsin. Most of the time, they were from an African nation, but occasionally we met students from India or Pakistan.

They were usually men, always people of color, with stories to share about where they were from and how they celebrated holidays different from America. Though in my youth, I didn't always recognize the value; these were interesting cultural exchanges of information and ideas that have probably played more influence and significance on who I have become, than I have given them credit for.

With Aunt Erma, there was never a time that couldn't turn into a learning time. I had hoped Aunt Erma and Uncle Leonard would be there for my children, to provide these same extraordinary moments of life beyond the norm. Before my children had a chance to know them, they were gone from this earth, much too soon. And unfortunately, there was just no suitable replacement for the people or the experience.

## Stay a While With Me

During these summers that my sister, brother and I spent in Wisconsin, we not only visited with our aunt and uncle, we also had pet ducks we visited with too, three of them. There was one for my brother, the biggest one; one for my sister, the littlest one; and one more for me in the middle. Those ducks miraculously never seemed to age from year to year. How do you suppose they managed that? Maybe JACK knows!

Uncle Leonard liked to hunt which meant we were used to eating game, including ducks. Did they eat our ducks and buy new ones every year? To this day, no one has risked asking JACK if he knows! At this point, I don't really want to know. Aunt Erma and Uncle Leonard were parents to the three of us every summer for two weeks. Sometimes they tried to convince us we should stay a third week, but we balked, thinking our parents would miss us too much.

After raising two children myself, I now recognize that those two to three week vacations for us were really about "vacations" for our parents "from us". Parents need vacations too. Before you can blink, it's Labor Day and back to school.

## Ebony and Ivory

In 1958, the year Foster Elementary School burned in a fire, my sister was in the 4th grade. I had already graduated and begun 7th grade at Skiles Junior High. Junior High was when we left the security of our immediate neighborhoods and friends from elementary school and ventured off to new experiences. It was our first experience with integrated classrooms. It was not, however, our first experience with integrated activities, as many of us had attended integrated summer programs and camps in and out of our community.

My junior high was newly built on the west side of town, lending itself to a population that would be largely black and Jewish. The Jewish population was mostly derived from attendance areas in neighboring Skokie, a suburb west of Evanston. The size of this population afforded us the opportunity to celebrate both Christian and Jewish holidays! We smugly thought we were ahead of the game when it came to integration.

Because of the extent of the damage caused by the fire at Foster, my sister had to grow through this loss of security experience at the tender age of nine. She finished her school year at Noyes elementary school, which was partially integrated due to earlier integrated housing patterns prior to the western Evanston migration. This year, for her, was not nearly as unforgettable as the 5th grade would be at Willard School.

The 5th grade for Foster pupils was spent in make shift classrooms in the basement of Willard. The Foster students were kept intact and not integrated into the regular Willard classrooms. This could have been a perfect opportunity to come together as a community. It didn't happen. Even lunch was separate. After lunch, however, all students were allowed on the playground for recess.

The Willard children were not allowed to mix or mingle with the Foster children. Can you imagine telling children not to play with each other? Those that broke "the rules" were sent to the principal's office. This had lasting effects on both the black and white children who, for the most part, innocently did not understand why. There was one anomaly at Willard school, a black gym teacher, Mrs. Jean Hunter. How that happened, no one can explain today.

She was like an angel sent from heaven for the Foster students. She looked like us and she understood. Tap dance, as part of gym class, was one of the new experiences she taught. Most of the students at Foster had never experienced this, especially not in gym class and no one had tap shoes. She showed the students how to improvise!

You go to the hardware store and buy the smooth metal guards that are intended for the bottom of furniture legs to minimize the scratching of the floor. Place one at the toe and one at the heel of your gym shoes and voila, you have tap shoes! They sounded so cool, no one wanted to take them off. This would be the first of many new and different experiences for the Foster children at Willard. Lessons, good and bad, are learned in the midst of adversity.

By the 6th grade, Foster was rebuilt and the black children returned to where they "belonged", but this would be the beginning of the end of the way things were. It was never quite the same after the fire. Eventually Foster became a Lab school and bussing for integration began.

Our community was home to one very large high school, Evanston Township High School, or E.T.H.S for short. It was a huge and stately campus, looking more like a college than a high school. Everyone just referred to it as "the high school" or "the big house". Ironically, the high school was located in the west side of Evanston; again, where most of Evanston's African American population resided. So it was the white kids who were bussed in, so to speak.

Actually, most of them took the city bus until, as seniors, they were allowed to drive their fancy cars and park in the parking lot that was just for students. My immediate friends and I lived about four blocks from the high school, so we walked, rain or shine, hot or biting cold.

Walking to school was a "chain" event. I left home at about 7:45 a.m., walked around the corner and picked up Dana; crossed the street and three houses down, picked up my cousin Cheryl; turned left at Lyons and traveled about a block, where we met Sharon on the corner of Hartrey and Church Streets. From here, we had about one and a half blocks to go and we were there at "the big house", our high school, E.T.H.S.

On the way we would pass by the football stadium. Even empty, you could hear the roar of the crowd and the band playing, "ETHS, we will fight for you, for the right to do, everything for you..." The football stadium was where we spent most Saturday mornings from late September through November. Sunshine or cold, not wind or rain, kept us from the game. "V i c t o r y comes while we

sing da da da…many trophies we will bring…so cheer, cheer!…"
Those were the days!

Over four thousand students attended our high school, with over
nine hundred in my graduating class of 1964 alone. By comparison,
my graduating class was about the same size of most entire high
schools, then and now. Everyone in town attended this high school,
except for the few that attended Catholic or private schools. Our
school was rich in culture, basically taken for granted. Whites,
Asians, Hispanics and African Americans, all under one roof of the
big house, gave the appearance of successful integration.

Ironically, even today, some forty years later, the honors classes are
still mostly white and Asian, and the remedial classes are dispro-
portionately filled with students of color. The lunchroom is still
largely separated by race, and racially inclusive social events are
minimally successful. I think we were more "integrated" in the
sixties than even now. At least, we worked at it. Integration was a
goal, a dream, a moral obligation.

## Always and Forever

My sister, brother and I were second-generation graduates from
E.T.H.S. My father and his brothers and sisters had attended during
the 1930's and 40's. So, the high school, in theory, had been "integrated" for some time. In practice, the high school was more
desegregated than successfully integrated. It was more something
that accidentally happened, rather than a purposeful event. It appears
from generation to generation, things related to race improve, plateau,
and then revert backward.

The 60's were a tumultuous time as African Americans were
fighting for civil rights in the South, with some spilling over in the
North. We complacently thought we were ahead of the game being
already "integrated". So it seemed. Evanston wasn't overtly hostile
and we didn't feel a great deal of discomfort. The support of our
parents made all the difference in the world. They shielded us from

racially intense situations and developed within us a sense of equality and pride.

Our parents were the ones who encouraged us to attend college, to achieve, to be successful. The counseling staff and many of the teachers at the high school assumed our futures did not include higher education and thus did not focus us in that direction. Those students who had attendance problems or appeared to under-perform academically, were actually encouraged to quit school.

Naively, we didn't view this as racist. Suggestions given for our future occupations were not of a professional nature. Aim low was the message. Adults in a child's life: Do they really know all there is to know?

## We've Only Just Begun

We instinctively knew where we were welcome to participate and what was reserved for white students only, the so-called majority race. It was not necessary to post signs. For example, plays were reserved for mainly white students, unless you were incredibly talented. I remember Mary Cheeks, an African American student, once getting the lead in the annual school musical. She probably had the most gifted voice in the entire town. The play director, Mr. Dixon, had to give her the part. To exclude her would have been too obvious, as no one had a thimble full of her talent.

We, never the less, persevered in our attempt for inclusiveness, and with some successes, "Firsts", as we called them during the Civil Rights era. We had the First black president of the school student council; first black cheerleader; first to write for the yearbook and school newspaper; first black homecoming queen, and so forth. You would think by now, forty years later, that students of any ethnic background could equitably compete for these and other opportunities. That is still not the case.

Times have changed. Now when we return for a reunion football game, the school appears to be 80% black. It isn't. Where have the white football fans gone? We see several young black girls with their babies bouncing on their laps; cheerleading squads with now a "token" white girl grinding cheers with a BET "flava". There are very few white athletes, at least playing football.

The African-American population hasn't grown that much, but with the newer Jamaican and Haitian populations, one would assume that the school is predominately black. It is my understanding, that by adding the Latinos to the mix, E.T.H.S. is approximately forty seven percent minority today. I'm pleasantly surprised when I meet a white parent who tells me that their kids are attending "the high school". I immediately think "how liberal"; these must be "good" people, Democrats!

I guess you have to know where to look. My sister does volunteer work for the Art of Makin' Music Foundation in Evanston. In September 2004 (forty years after I entered E.T.H.S.), the foundation hosted a full day field trip for the high school orchestra and chorus at Joy Art recording studio. You could count the number of African-American participants and volunteers on one hand, out of the fifty-four participants.

In this setting, one would assume that "the high school" is eighty percent white! So much for desegregation vs. integration, because after all this time, we've still only just begun.

## Games People Play

Now sports, we could do, then and now. We were not excluded from this opportunity, at least not in my high school educational lifetime. Most of America has learned the lesson, that winning is more important than racism. And of course, winning is all about money. If there's one thing this country worships more than God, it is money. So athletics have helped to break down some of the barriers to equal opportunity.

Black and white coaches were supportive and quite influential to the success of both black and white athletes at E.T.H.S. Athletic scholarships helped as well, but without a good coach standing by, only the extremely gifted athlete was guaranteed the opportunity of a scholarship.

Case in point: Rick, a white student from a financially modest background, interestingly credits his black high school track coach with encouraging him to attend college. Neither of his parents had attended college or graduated high school. None of his teachers had encouraged post- graduate study, as his grades were at best, mediocre. It was Mr. Thomas, his black coach, who inspired him and gave him the courage to apply. Today, he is a college graduate and a successful businessman.

Many coaches, like Mr. Thomas, were substitute parents and mentors to the male athletes. I refer to them as old school coaches. They were a saving grace for many boys who had become disenfranchised by the educational system. During reminiscent discussions of high school days, the male discussion inevitably leads to fond memories of athletic teams and coaches.

Unfortunately, during the sixties, there weren't many girls' teams, so the same mentoring opportunity for girls was nonexistent. It was not like today, at least not during school. We were the pre-Title IX generation. I remember playing on a girls' softball team during the summer, but the season was short and relationships short-term.

This was not really a problem for us girls, as we seemed to have "mothers" everywhere. Growing up in my world, everybody's mother had "license" to be your "outside" mother. Witnessed public misbehavior could be corrected by any adult present, and it was likely that by the time I reached home, my mother would have already been informed.

## Still the One
Still, attending Evanston schools gave African American students a leg up. We had excellent teachers for the most part and an excellent curriculum. If you took advantage of the opportunity, you were well prepared for college or any chosen vocation. Our educational

requirements were strict and challenging. In each of the four years of high school English, we were required to write a research paper, my favorite part of the curriculum. In addition, we were required to do scholarly readings. By the time I attended college, writing and doing research was second nature to me.

Our college roommates from other schools often struggled with producing lengthy term papers. As graduates of "the high school", most of us completed those assignments effortlessly.In fact, if the majority of the grade was based on a written paper, I knew I had the course aced. The first two years at NIU, the flunk out years for most, were not the challenge that I feared nor expected.

Only biology and psychology proved to be difficult subjects. My psychology teacher was a Hungarian woman with a heavy accent. Every Monday, Wednesday and Friday, I spent two hours of listening to what sounded like nonsense to me. I never understood two consecutive words she said. It's too bad they don't provide those interpreter headsets like they do at the United Nations. I could have used a set.

Dr. Whatever-her-name-was's, lecture never seemed to relate to our textbook either. I tried to take copious notes and then find the related text after class. That proved to be a fruitless effort. My class-mates were always asking her the proverbial question, "Is this going to be on the test?" There was never a clear-cut answer. It was diffi-cult to know what was critical to know and study, thus, the resulting "D" in Psychology; and my only "D" in undergraduate study. Biology was a success story I will discuss later.

Imperfect as it was, there was something special about growing up in Evanston. Is anywhere perfect? Actually, in some instances, inte-gration worked well, like the Girl Scout troop we belonged to. Our adult leader was an African American mother, but the troop membership was a combination of black, white and Jewish girls. We worked together, sang songs around a campfire, ate "smores", and learned plenty about each other while earning badges.

Those experiences shaped us. They shaped our future, our politics. It was part of the culture of our community to volunteer and share with others, not even realizing how little we had ourselves, as we were rich in much more than money and material things.

## The Power of Love

Doing well in school, for me, did not happen because of the support I received from many of my high school teachers. Success was expected at home, not an option. It's interesting how you remember the best and worst teachers of your educational experience. Some years are a complete blur to me. I remember nothing of the third and fourth grades, not the teachers or anything that happened. It is as if someone erased those years from my memory.

My most absolutely, unforgettable teachers were my first and second grade teachers, Mrs. Hunter and Miss. Harvey. They were great. Some of the worst I've ever had, you will meet later. I prefer to start with the best. Mrs. Hunter and Miss. Harvey were both African American teachers at Foster elementary school, where I attended from kindergarten through the sixth grade. They both held their students to a high standard and provided us the love and encouragement needed to reach it. They were the embodiment of "TLC", before TLC became a popular and overused acronym.

As a shy, young child, I lacked confidence. Because I tended to be rather quiet, it would have been easy to overlook me in class. They never did. Miss Harvey and Mrs. Hunter made me feel like I was smart and could achieve anything, if I worked hard. They basically treated all their students that way, and somehow made you individually feel special, at the same time.

When Mrs. Hunter called on me in class, it resembled a Bill Clinton "you are the only person I see in the room" moment that made me feel like I was the most special student of her entire career. She had a soft and endearing smile that was infectious. She was confident that I would have the correct answer, even if it wasn't so.

It was not uncommon, in our small community, to encounter current and former teachers at community events, or just shopping at the grocery store. I remember on one occasion, while attending a tea at the Unitarian Church, Miss Harvey introduced me to a group of her friends. She referred to me as her very "best student" in the second grade. I knew even at my young age that there were smarter students than me in her class. Never the less, I felt delightfully embarrassed and proud at the same time. If she had that much faith in me, perhaps I should have more confidence and belief in my potential as well. Her words still inspire me today.

## Something Tells Me I'm into Something Good

There were a few other quality teachers sprinkled throughout my academic career. Most notably, Mr. Joseph Hill, who began as my gym teacher at Foster School and later became the superintendent of the Evanston Elementary School District #65. He was among the greats. Even from the beginning of our relationship, he wasn't just a physical education teacher. He was a mentor and taught me a lot of life's lessons as well. Folk and square dancing, alternately, were part of our P.E. curriculum every year. Though we learned the steps, it wasn't just about the dance. It was about recognizing and respecting other cultures, as well.

Equally important, it was about accepting each other, our differences and working together. Ultimately, the music and dances we practiced, all culminated into a performance before a live audience. It was beautiful. Sometimes we even wore costumes. During dance rehearsals, we had to hold hands, actually touching our partners, as part of the dance routines. Of course at ten and eleven years old, there was some level of discomfort with this. The boys would act unusually silly, if that's possible, and always had sweaty hands.

We usually had the opportunity to choose our partners. The same people habitually made the same choices, so sometimes Mr. Hill made choices for us. More often than I liked, my partner was Roosevelt Jones. Roosevelt was neglected at home, coming from poor circumstances. This I surmised, as I never actually knew where he lived or visited there. His clothes were always dirty and he smelled pretty bad too. I almost passed out every time he raised his arm at the call of "swing your partner".

Nobody wanted to be his partner, including me. Somehow, just a look from Mr. Hill and I knew it was my turn to choose Roosevelt for my partner. That made Roosevelt happier than I ever imagined. He flashed a big toothy grin before grabbing my arm. Mr. Hill recognized, at the time, how important learning tolerance and being open minded was. I still wished that, once in a while, I could end up with the cute boy in class!

That lesson didn't hit home until it was time to dance with partners in junior high, our first experience with social integration. There were white students in our class who didn't want to choose the black students as partners, and we didn't smell bad either. I now knew first hand how Roosevelt felt back in grade school. Things improved as time went on and we became accustomed and even friendly with each other.

Beyond skin color, we learned we were not so different after all. Kids need to grow up together to learn that lesson. It's much harder to learn as an adult. I was amused by the post- Spring break conversations of the white students, as they bragged about and expressed pride in their "acquired tans"; tans as a result of trips to Florida or some Caribbean island. They would place their forearms next to mine, as the standard of measure. Whoever managed to tan darker than me was the proud winner. They wanted to be brown like us, but they didn't want to be us!

## The Bad, What Kind of Fool Do You Think I Am?

The first time in my life I ever received a "C" in English was my freshman year in high school. I had the misfortune of being assigned to Ms. Blum for English the first semester. Some teachers assume that because you have graduated from an all black school, you can't possibly be as prepared as one should be for the next level, whether it is high school or college. The assumption is that black students possess an inferior gene pool to begin with, compounded by inferior curriculum taught by the least qualified teachers, inevitably resulting in lack of preparedness for high school, or whatever the pursuit might be.

My husband experienced this same attitude in his Freshman College English class at Northwestern University. His professor insisted that because he was a graduate of the Chicago Public Schools, there was no way he could achieve or receive a grade above a "D". In an effort to prove him wrong, my husband foolishly enrolled in this professor's English class for three consecutive semesters and he received three undeserved "Ds". The prophecy is fulfilled.

At the first parent conference in the fall semester of my freshman year, Mrs. Blum enlightened my father that she had "…given out no A's and a lot of shaky B's and B minus's, and I had earned a good solid C+." Now isn't that special? "What did it matter anyway?" She would continue to say with her cat-shaped, rhinestone glasses, slid half way down her pointed nose, "whether it was a 'B' or a 'C.'" The grade was only important for calculating grade point averages, affecting those students who plan to attend college; and, she didn't expect I would be attending college.

Lord, I thought my father was going to reach across the table and choke the life out of the woman (an action I had on occasion fantasized myself). I had never seen him so angry. How dare she make that assumption! His eyes were red and his nostrils flared as wide as saucers. "My children are going to college and I'll buy every damn book in this school if that's what they need", my father said. By the time he was finished, she was speechless and no longer smiling.

I'm smiling outside, but I'm thinking inside, next time it will probably be a "D+"! She probably hates me now. Needless to say, he had me removed from her class and I never received less than a "B" in English again. I don't know how he managed that miracle, as it was a rare occasion that the principal allowed a parent to make a class change based on not liking the teacher.

Oh, to have been a fly on the wall during that discussion between my dad and the principal. If he hadn't accomplished that mission, I might not be writing this book today. Mrs. Blum would have most certainly killed my love of writing like my Science teachers did for the subject of Science.

## And the Ugly, That's Life

Some teachers don't realize how uninviting they can be to the educational process. For instance, I would have majored in the field of Science were it not for not one, but three, idiot Science teachers I endured from sixth grade through my freshman year in college. First, there was Mrs. Whitemore, my sixth grade teacher. She used to ask the class if we wanted to do Science or go outside for recess!

What kind of choice was that? Who was the adult in the room? I was the lone vote for Science. Nice lady with a real nice smile and dimples, but, I think she was afraid of Science. My pragmatic experience, as a veteran teacher, reveals that many elementary teachers are. Unless they were Science-focused as undergraduate students, the content was avoided like the plague. Even I avoided Science classes beyond the minimum requirements. The minimum requirements tended to be met in most teaching curriculums at college and universities.

Science content can be harder to teach than, say, English. Thus, most of the time Science is taught as a reading comprehension class. Read the chapter and answer the questions at the end. Boring! And skip the challenge question, which usually requires an experiment. The required materials for the experiment were non-existent. Science ought to be more experimental, with hands on activities, but then that would require more knowledge, understanding, money and certainly more preparation.

## And the Ugly, Then Came You

My 7th grade Science teacher, Mr. Stickman, should have sought another career. Nothing about him was suitable for junior high teaching; not his size, his temperament or the sound of his voice. Teaching was simply not his calling. The poor man was nice, but had no control over the class behavior or attention. His teaching style lacked what was necessary to motivate students and hold their interest.

Mr. Stickman was a small man, not much taller than we were, weighed about 110 pounds and had a gold-capped front tooth. I think he was probably gay, but we didn't discuss, much less emphasize such things then. That was too personal. Mr. Stickman's idiocy is obvious in the next example of an absurd but, sad and true story. The names have been changed to protect the innocent!

It was a warm, spring day. I could feel a slight breeze blowing on the back of my neck from the windows behind us. It felt really good, as the cool morning had left me overdressed for the afternoon. Our desks faced forward, toward one of two blackboards and a bulletin board in the classroom, to minimize distractions from outside. Truth be known, there was more science happening outside the window, than ever happened in that classroom.

Per the daily routine, Howie, the class clown, left a thumbtack in the seat of Mr. Stickman's chair. We sat quietly chatting, awaiting Mr. Stickman's arrival with the bell. With the ringing, arrived two late students who ran through the door and quickly slid into their desks, while Mr. Stickman followed very quietly behind. His slight build allowed him to approach so lightly afoot, that unless we were watching, we never heard him enter the classroom.

He would begin to talk and write with chalk on the board, usually the chapter number we were to read and discuss from the textbook. There were very few hands-on experiments, which Mr. Stickman avoided, as the result was usually more chaos than he could handle. Quiet reading, with some lecture, led to a great deal of boredom and sometimes-bad behavior. Actually, we were pretty good kids compared to today's standards!

We didn't bring drugs, guns and knives to school; mostly tacks, candy, gum and once in a while a New York deli style dill pickle. And while there may have been loud talking, there was never fighting inside the building.

So Howie has put this tack in the teacher's chair again today. With perspiration beginning to run down our foreheads, we wait for Mr. Stickman to sit. My mouth is dry, as I think this will be the day Mr. Stickman will blow a gasket and really let us have it! Howie is the perpetrator, but we are all guilty by association. I'm thinking that we'll be in detention the rest of our lives for not warning him.

He sits. For crying out-loud, the man sits on the thumbtack and says nothing. One time, he sits, then again and again. This happens every day. Most of the time he doesn't even remove the tack. So he stands up to write on the chalkboard, and there it is. That silver tack attached to the back of his grey pinstriped suit coat, all shiny and sparkling from any view in the classroom. Surely he had felt that! Didn't he? He would sit down again with the tack attached to the back of his coat.

He never said a word. We're counting the number of sittings and missing the Science lesson, as this is a major distraction. I bet he went home most days with a butt that looked like a pincushion, with little tiny red dots on his skinny, white butt. We didn't learn much most days, too focused on what he might say or do. He never acknowledged what Howie had done, so I don't know why day after day I expected him to. Why didn't he just deal with it? After a while, Howie found something else stupid to do. He had an endless supply of brainless ideas for wasting time in class.

## Ball of Confusion

Stupid is as stupid does…or so the saying goes. Mr. Stickman is as Mr. Stickman does, which most times left us a bit confused as to what to expect. Occasionally, Mr. Stickman would deal with inappropriate behavior in the class, but only minor infractions like the following. We were sitting in Science class one really sweltering Friday afternoon, taking a test that we should have taken on Thursday, but Mickey had successfully applied the usual delay tactic of asking Mr. Stickman a question.

Each time before he would pass out the tests, Mr. Stickman would say with that toothy grin of his, "Are there any questions before we begin?". That was Mickey's cue to waste enough time so that the test could not be given in that class period. So, now we have one more night to study, but who likes taking tests on Fridays? Who was really hurt here? Not Stickman.

At any rate, on Friday, the next day during the test, my friend, Eric, is gazing out the window at class 7-11 playing baseball during their Gym period. After a moment or two, he turned his head back and started talking with a classmate. He was already finished with the test and it was too hot to sleep. Within seconds, he felt a sudden sharp pain in his right ear and let out a rather girlie scream! It was Mr. Stickman inflicting that pain. Who knew he had that kind of strength.

He came up from behind and snatched the top of the Eric's right ear, pulling him upward and physically out of the desk. Through clenched teeth, Mr. Stickman was able to utter in a fiercely "quiet" manner to the student, "You are distracting your classmates. Sit quietly and finish the exam." Now this was most uncharacteristic for Mr. Stickman, who usually ignored really bad behavior, but on this occasion had decided to challenge a minor infraction.

They looked tensely at each other in that old western film "show down" format. We waited to see who would draw first. Then it was over as quickly as it started. The student, who was twice the size of Mr. Stickman, just looked at him and sat down rubbing his ear. I think the shock of it all just wouldn't allow an immediate response. Looking back, Mr. Stickman was passive, somewhat peculiar at times.

Perhaps on this particular day, he was still feeling the sting of that tack in his butt, or maybe it was just too damn hot and he would rather be playing baseball like the rest of us. At any rate, a friendlier reprimand would have made the point, and then again…I felt sorry for the man. I can't remember what came next. Nor do I remember much of what we learned that year while sitting in 7th grade Science class. Even worse, I can't remember 8th grade Science at all, not even the teacher's name.

## What'd I Say?

I saved the best (worst) for last. Mr. Jenson, my college freshman year Biology professor, was the most "uninviting" of any teacher I can recall. As a predictor of success in his class, this idiot gave the entire class a pretest on the very first day. The results were not used to inform his instruction as it related to the needs of the students. Quite the contrary, our scores were used as a predictor of probable grades we would receive at the end of the semester. I imagine, he assumed and wanted us to agree, that one test could predict how successful (well unsuccessful) we would be in his class.

This was another self-fulfilling prophecy theory at work. He had been giving the test so long that his theory was proved fairly accurate. Or, maybe his attitude and teaching helped to provide the results he expected. He was such an arrogant man, considering himself most brilliant. If he was so smart, why wasn't he in some research lab somewhere discovering the cure for cancer, instead of teaching hormone-loaded and easily intimidated college freshmen?

Considering my previous experiences with Science teachers, I was not the most prepared student in class. So yep, I was scientifically calculated to receive a big, fat "D" from Mr. Jenson. One third of the class, the chicken third, dropped out in the second week, but I like a challenge. So tag, Mr. Jenson, you're "it". Nobody was going to tell Arlene Yvonne Avery, the granddaughter of Mary Elizabeth Avery, she was destined to receive a "D" based on some pretest. Psychology was already a losing proposition so I could ill afford another one.

By the end of the semester, I earned an "A" in Biology 101. Idiot number three, Mr. Jenson, offered me the opportunity to major in Biology, as he was so impressed with my ability. That is what he actually wrote to me in a two page, typed letter. It was much too late. I was flattered, but proudly declined. I had won and moved on. He didn't know JACK.

By the way, my grandmother, Mary Elizabeth Avery, was known for her "never let anybody push you around" attitude. My father, her first born, was a lot like her in that respect. We used to joke that whenever we had to be strong, we simply displayed the "Mary Elizabeth syndrome". I had to explain the concept to my boss, who had seen Mary Elizabeth emerge from my psyche one day in the office, and wasn't quite sure how to handle "her".

It is a kind of "don't mess with me" thing we inherited; that self-confidence we didn't know we had until we were much older. My boss questioned me about the "look" on my face and some posturing I had done that she wasn't quite comfortable with. "What look?" I asked. She imitated my behavior back to me and I had to laugh. "Oh that's just my grandmother", I replied. "She emerges from below the surface every now and then."

## Call it De Ja Vu

Idiots don't just teach Science. They exist in Math courses too. Though Math was never my favorite subject, I did very well. At the end my 8th grade year, Mr. Calumbo, my Math teacher, recommended me for high school General Math, instead of Algebra. As far as I was concerned, I had just completed general Math in the 8th grade, while others no brighter than me accomplished pre-Algebra. This would not only be a repeat for me as a freshman, but a bad recommendation for a college-bound student.

With one year wasted, there wouldn't be time to take Algebra, Geometry and Trigonometry or Algebra 3, all requirements for entry into college, not to mention the ACT test. I felt like I was the only kid in his class he did that to. I wasn't, of course. Most of the black students received this treatment. Mr. Calumbo had no academic reason to recommend me for General Math. I had received excellent grades in his class, but I was rather shy and quiet, so he may have mistaken that for something else. Surely he wasn't guilty of the "R" word that Americans pretend doesn't exist any more.

I used to raise my hand in his class all the time. I knew the answers. He would look directly at me and then call on another student. That can make you want to stop raising your hand altogether. Giving the correct answer, to be validated by the teacher in front of the other students, builds confidence. It makes you feel really good about yourself. In other words, able to be competitive and win. After being ignored a while, I began to wonder if it mattered, knowing the answer. I felt invisible.

Once again, my parents had to get involved. Sometimes schools base too much on teachers' opinions. With my parents' encouragement, I took Algebra instead and earned an "A" in both semesters. Algebra was a piece of cake.

## You Don't Remember Me, But I Remember You

When school was out for the summer of 1961, I went back to my junior high, ostensibly to tell Mr. Calumbo how wrong he had been about me. He was gone. Damn, I was ready for him too. He was no longer teaching at the junior high. Maybe he found a new career for which he was better suited, and saved those who followed me a lot of grief. I really, really wanted to tell him what I thought of him. Well, more like how wrong he had been about me, and kiss my ass too.

Not really. I didn't have that kind of courage then. I bet he doesn't even remember me, but I remember him. It's been forty plus years and that experience is still on my mind. See how powerful an effect teachers can have on you, on your children?

Teachers have a lot of power. Some abuse or misuse that power to the detriment of many students. My brother-in-law, who also graduated from "the high school", was elected president of Combined Studies by his fellow peers, freshman year. He accepted with pride and a sense of accomplishment. The teacher took him aside after class and convinced him that it was best to relinquish the position.

It was a devastating experience. So painful that he never told his dad, his mom, nor any other living soul, until he finally shared the experience with his wife of twenty five years. Imagine the effect baggage like that has on your confidence. There actually *are* experiences that you just can't "get past". Another black classmate, who had less than stellar grades at "the high school", including a D in accounting, was also discouraged from reaching for higher goals.

Maybe he was immature, or a late bloomer, or the product of inferior instruction for the first six grades. Regardless of the reason, his teachers did not have high expectations for him. His first move after passing the CPA exam, upon graduation from college, was to go back "looking" for Mr. Jones, his accounting teacher, to rub it in his face. It felt genuinely good, like he could breathe for the first time in a long time.

## Pick Up the Pieces

Parents have a lot of power too, though they don't always exercise it appropriately, and unfortunately, sometimes not at all. I've known some adults for whom school was so painful that they cannot bear to walk the halls again, not even for their own children. Parents should question teachers and administrators. They have the right to challenge decisions that teachers make regarding the placement of their children in academic "tracks" and even the grades given.

It's a delicate balance though, as parents whose actions are too aggressive, can cause a worse situation for their children. I've seen some parents today who perhaps lack the verbal ability to express their pain and displeasure appropriately. They end up cursing or threatening the teacher.

This serves no positive purpose. Rather than an improved behavior and attitude towards the child, the result may be that the teacher becomes more hostile and less supportive. It's unprofessional, but consciously or unconsciously, the teacher writes the child off because of feelings toward the parent. My girlfriends in the field of social work have witnessed this phenomenon, unfortunately, much too often. Both the parent and the teacher have forgotten how important the other is.

Love is not enough. Parents must find ways to help build and maintain their children's self esteem. Self-esteem is that inner voice that tells you that you can or cannot accomplish a goal. If that inner voice is feeling confident and strong, it will get you through adversity, through the naysayers, past the "NO". Low self-esteem allows you to blame others for your failure, to find reasons to give up, to stop short of reaching your full potential.

If there is one skill you need in today's workplace, it is "kick ass confidence". There's no room for weak people. Successful people don't quit, don't give up, they find another way. They play to win every time.

## One in a Million

Even though today many of them live miles away, I still feel close to my childhood girlfriends. When we see each other, it's as if the years haven't passed. We see each other through the same youthful eyes. You know, young, beautiful, carefree, no gray hair and fifty pounds thinner, riding our bikes through the neighborhood tirelessly, endlessly looking for other friends or whoever was the "cutest" boy on the block that week!

We had not yet experienced the pain of a broken heart, any major disappointments or any REAL responsibility. We had our chores around the house that had to be completed before going on the "ride". Looking back on it, that was nothing compared to managing your own household, your own life. Don't be afraid to look back. It may help you move forward. But don't get stuck there! You have to learn to deal with the hand that life has dealt you. But at some point, when the time is right, don't be afraid to reshuffle the deck. You can deal yourself another hand. I have, more than once.

As I have already said, hold tight to your girlfriends. They may save your life one day in ways you'd never imagine at the age of nine. Girlfriends are there for you when that first love breaks your heart. What would you do if they weren't there to reassure you how worthless he was in the first place? Years later, my girlfriend Annie, would grocery shop for my elderly mother who lived sixty miles away from me. That was wonderful help to my mother and a great comfort to me.

We looked out for each other as kids and adults. As adults, some of us were as close with our classmates' parents, as we were with our classmates. We would think nothing of helping to take care of each other's parents, as necessary. You see, we are baby-boomers. We are children of the sixties. Products of old school love.

That's the kind of love that says you belong to me even if you are the neighbor's kid. This was the kind of love that would correct you when you did wrong and then tell your parents too. The kind of love that makes you do right, even when you think nobody is watching, because you know somebody is always watching. And everybody watching knows your mama *and* your daddy.

My kids, for the most part, don't even know the parents of their friends; don't really care like we did. That old school love just wasn't there for them in the same way as it was for us, not even in Jack and Jill. This might be the unfortunate result of the mobile society in which they have grown up. Our neighborhoods were stable. Theirs changed frequently.

Childhood, as we're going through it, seems as though it will last forever. Then before we realize it, we're leaving the neighborhood; our many friends; comforts and protections we've grown accustomed to, for the *unknown*. We're off to college.

College was a whole new world. I remember, traveling to visit my brother in college at Southern Illinois University in Carbondale, Illinois, which is located at the very southern tip of Illinois, and about a six-hour drive from our home. It may as well have been in the mountains of Kentucky. The town's people had thick southern accents, dressed like farmers and behaved similar to people I had seen in movies about poor share croppers. They stared at us like we were from another planet.

At the time, I thought little of it. Encountering unfriendly white folks was not a new phenomenon. We, initially, had a wonderful visit on campus, attending a football game and a homecoming party. Exhausted, we decided to spend the night before embarking on the long drive home. As we stopped from one motel to another, curiously, they were all "full". That's believable the first and maybe even the second time it happens, but six times?

We had to drive all the way back to St. Louis before we found a place that would allow black customers lodging. I never realized this until I was an adult. I just thought my dad liked to keep driving to get as close to home as possible before stopping. Life goes by while you are asleep in the back of a car.

I thought adulthood would remain as childhood, easy and uncomplicated, just with more freedom and money. It seemed simple. You get a good job, your own car, an apartment and just have fun. The definition of fun is, do what you want, when you want, with whom you want, where you want. No cares in the world except what you want next!

I didn't realize, until much later in life, how hard my father worked to make my life seem simple. How much humiliation and discrimination both my parents endured, and sheltered us kids from it, to keep our childhood innocent and happy.

# Cynthia

## It Ain't Necessarily So

"Cream rises to the top", or so we are told, and I once believed. But, it ain't necessarily so. With the Yale flunk out, and the Yale marginal graduate running the country today (pick any day between 2000 and 2006), or shall we say running it into the ground, the contradiction is obvious. Privileged people, especially sons, start at the top because of who their daddy is or what their daddy does. It certainly does influence who gets into Harvard and Yale. It is the most effective form of affirmative action there is.

I've learned that cream rising to the top is a myth of childhood, used as a motivational tool for children. And as such, it's not bad. For its time, it provided a good visual image for us children of the sixties. At my elementary school, beginning in second grade, every child with a permission slip could take a musical instrument lesson during lunch for no charge.

This was someone's idea of bringing piano lessons to the colored school. The music students throughout the decades were good, bad or mediocre, and some were declared prodigies. Where are they now? Where are those who were named the cream of the crop? Are they at the top? Of course, today's kids would probably think cream, and see a purple and white carton of Half and Half.

Would they consider Jessica and Ashley Simpson prodigies? Is that an example of cream rising to the top? On the other hand, what about James Brown? As you get older, it's important to be able to recognize real cream from buttermilk. Now some people like buttermilk. I think it tastes sour. Don't be fooled by the likeness to cream. There's a big difference.

# Carla

## 'Twas Not So Long Ago

I'm the first generation that didn't follow the path led by my grandmother; having to do day work as a life profession. Though she was a graduate of the Miss Mary Holmes finishing school, my grandmother did day work until her death. She was literate and possessed all the acceptable social graces, except it didn't matter, as more professional jobs were not available to her.

Black women were maids and childcare providers, some with degrees, earned mostly in the South. With migration North, the typical jobs available were for housework duties. Our grandmothers sometimes put in fourteen-hour days for the mistress, before returning home to care for their own families. That care of their own families usually took place after dark and before daybreak. The children raised by these women, our mothers and grandmothers, benefited from their knowledge and upbringing, long before it was recognized.

My mother initially started down this path and was able to exit upon earning a degree. Finally, education was starting to pay off in the black community. She continued further and earned a Masters Degree also. Black American women were super-nannies of white children long before the popularization of the British super-nanny on TV today. They raised some pretty good children. Look what has happened since we have returned that task to their real mothers!

## There Was a Time

I remember my third grade teacher at Noyes school, Mrs. Cuffe, like it was yesterday. In the third grade, it's pretty black and white. Either you can spell, read and do Math, or you can't. There is very little subjectivity that can enter into the equation. I was a straight A student and one of only three black students in a class of twenty-two. There wasn't anything that I couldn't do well. Everyone recognized that fact, even the other students in the class.

Toward the end of the school year, it was the practice of Mrs. Cuffe to list on the chalkboard the names of those students who would be moving up to the fourth grade. Not everyone made the list. As a quiet, well behaved, doing what you are supposed to do student earning A's, I had reason to believe that my name would not only make the list, but be at the top of the list.

Frankly, my name should have been the first name to grace the chalkboard. It wasn't, but I didn't worry. Not at first. Every day, the teacher added new names to the list. Mine was not one of them. Even the other children in the class knew my name should have been there. When the list included more than half the class itself, I told my mother.

I would soon discover that my mother, too, had survived Mrs. Cuffe in the third grade! Old habits die hard. At any rate, my mother immediately went to school and held what I can only assume today was a very "interesting" discussion with Mrs. Cuffe. The next day when I went to school, my name was on the list. My mother didn't mention racism. It wasn't in her vocabulary. She just went to the school and handled it.

Buried in that cruelty was the knowledge of knowing that I was qualified, and that waiting for things to be fair could take a lifetime. I've been holding, "holding back the years...holding back the tears".

## Only the Strong Survive

If this is what you experience everyday, it can undermine you. Being treated unfairly, for no reason, can push you to lose faith in yourself and the system; to become angry. Anger can be self destructive, as well. You may delay or fail to reach your own goals. You need to know who you are, so that other peoples' racism doesn't get in the way of your survival, of what you might otherwise accomplish. What could this lady, my teacher, really do to me? She couldn't lower my grades. She couldn't take away my brains, my thirst for knowledge, my love of books, or my pride. I would survive, despite the scar left in my heart.

In the 5th grade, we formed a social club for the sole purpose of having fun. The membership included several girls from my school. We held club meetings in each other's homes on no particular date and at no particular time. We would make doll clothes, cookies, talk and laugh a lot. Meetings were like "play dates" before such a phrase was coined during the Yuppie era. I was the only black girl in the club and it didn't seem to matter.

I felt comfortable in the homes of my white "girlfriends". No one ever expressed anything to make me feel unwelcome. When it was my turn to host a club meeting, I was very excited. My mother helped me shop for the right refreshments and clean the house so that everything would be perfect. I was so proud to have them come to my house.

On the day of club meeting, I waited and waited. Sadly, no one showed up. I thought, maybe, I had the date or something wrong. My mother made up some silly excuse, which I gladly accepted and went on as if nothing had happened. It wasn't until we planned a boy/girl party that I finally got the message. The other parents called and told my mother that I could not attend. I got the message, and learned the lesson in the message.

Years later, I realized how much the parents manipulated our environment. My white girlfriends had no idea how I had been treated by their parents. In fact, thirty years later at my high school reunion, as we reminisced about our club, one of my white classmates asked me, "How come we never went to your house?" The question was surprisingly genuine. Did she live in my world? Life is not fair. This is experienced by all people at one time or another. I choose to dust myself off, move on, to survive.

# Mavis

## Can I Get a Witness?

"Moms", as we called her, was a single parent and my mother. I think she had sex only two times in her life. Once, she got me, and the second time, she got my brother. After that, she gave up on men in her life. None of them stayed around long enough to claim responsibility or be of any support. She, never the less, was a survivor and my brother and I lived a decent, albeit frugal, life.

Moms worked hard as a domestic servant for a white woman who, herself, was a job loss away from poverty. I found it interesting that even poor white women of the fifties were able to employ domestic help. An entitlement at birth, I suppose. This also demonstrates how little people like my mother were paid.

At any rate, from this job, my mother saved and scrimped until she was able to buy a small brick bungalow on the south side of Chicago. We had high hopes from this purchase and dreams of much more. Well, as soon as her employer discovered that my mother had bought a home, Moms was fired. An entitlement not allowed at birth for us, in her employer's eyes anyway. This woman my moms worked for announced that she "couldn't believe my mother could buy a home off what she was paying her."

Did she think we didn't deserve a home? Did she think my mother was paid too much for the menial tasks she was doing? This white woman viewed herself a woman of good, moral, Christian values. She was a typical so-called upstanding member of the community. She's recently passed away while residing in a nursing home located in a politically named red state.

A red state is one that voted Republican, i.e., conservative Christian values, in the previous presidential election. What values did this woman's behavior truly represent? Our lives did not end with the experience of this woman, and I resolved early in my childhood that my life would not have the same fate. Of course, my mother couldn't afford to send us to college. She did teach my brother and me important survival skills and a belief in ourselves, which has served us well through adulthood.

# Annie

## What's Love Got to Do With It?

My parents were raised in deeply religious families. At least, they were taught to fear God, and maybe that means the same thing. I'm not sure. At any rate, I grew up with this history. We went to church every Sunday and prayed, and then prayed a lot at home. I believed in a power bigger than myself, who loved me and worked in my favor, though I wasn't always able to give witness to that fact.

As the second born in a family of five children, I had a lot of responsibility for my younger brothers and sisters. My family's income was marginal, so my mother had to work; leaving me with many of the household chores of cooking, cleaning and washing. Mom did day work like many other women of her age. She worked for the same family from the age of sixteen, until she was sixty. The job ended, and my mother retired when the old lady she worked for died.

I had an older sister, so most of my clothes were hand-me-downs. I didn't mind. They looked pretty good on me. Our family produced lots of dirty laundry, and as soon as I could reach the top of the washing machine, it was my job to do it. Sometimes I didn't get it all done, and I had to go to school with dirty clothes on. My teachers used to tell me I smelled bad and my clothes didn't match. My girl-friends never said such things to me, so I didn't believe the teachers. I didn't believe what the teachers said about my clothes anyway.

Another of my chores was to mop the kitchen floor everyday. My brothers and I would put the soap and water on the floor, and then take turns "ice skating" in our stocking feet across the floor, until it was clean. Mom always wondered how we could get our socks so dirty with shoes on! The things mothers don't know. Sometimes we played restaurant. We secretly opened cans of food, pretended to cook, and then put the cans back on the shelf.

That proved unwise on one occasion. After our "dinner", we rolled and taped paper bags together and pretended like we were smoking cigarettes. We had observed the adults doing that, smoking cigarettes, that is. Smoking "paper bags" was an activity that could really lead to trouble. Fortunately, we never burned the house down! But, with three brothers and a sister, lots of things can happen.

Days later, while reading the Bible at the kitchen table, mom smelled something awful. The open cans of decaying corn were bubbling over from the heat and oozing a foam-like substance. She was so angry with us, she cried! "Who opened these cans and wasted all this food?" We scattered like mice. Fortunately, there were no weapons in this Christian home. "Don't even ask to go anywhere for weeks, months, ever," she screamed through tears of pain and fear. Mom spent time on her knees that night. Me too!

We were on punishment until canned corn was once again on sale at the local Jewel grocery store. She sent me to the store with two dollars and fifteen cents to buy twenty cans of corn. "And bring me my change back, even if it's one penny", she said. To this day, I don't buy canned goods at the store. I'll eat anything except vegetables in a can.

Once we broke the front window while playing ball; something we were never to do in the front yard, of course. Our motto was to never admit to anything, which rarely worked, because mom would just whip all of us. That took a lot of time, since there were five of us. I tried to be last because she would be tired by then and I would get fewer licks.

Mom quit having children after my brother, Allen, was born. I guess there were becoming too many children to spank. I didn't know this at the time, but you can wear a mother out. One way or another, we survived our parenting, or maybe our parents survived us.

## Let the Good Times Roll

On sunny summer afternoons, my mother would give the five of us a blanket and card table and tell us to "play" in the back yard. We would be out there for hours; engaged in such fantasies as running our own restaurant, teaching school, attending church, or just playing house. We had pretend dishes, pretend books, pretend outfits, pretend food, pretend musical instruments, pretend everything. The card table and blanket served as multiple items, as needed, in our role-play.

Often dandelions, which we had plenty of in our yard, provided a variety of uses during afternoon pretend vocations. They were food, lovely flowers and even jewelry, when tied together and placed them around our necks. They served as "wedding bouquets", funeral arrangements, and gifts for the "teacher". Momma didn't know, but on some occasions we used her real dishes and silverware outside.

The big mixing spoon served us well as the microphone from the pulpit. The spoon also served momma well as a spanking instrument when nothing else was available.

## Ooh Child

One sunny Monday morning, I'd had a big breakfast of bacon, oatmeal and toast, a nice leisurely walk to school with my big sister. All was well with my world, until my first grade teacher called on me to read. I was ready to read on this particular morning, eager to read to my teacher and the class. I was feeling really good.

I started reading with normal six-year old speed which slowed to, I admit, a snails pace by page two. She stopped me in the middle of a paragraph. "Dana", she said. "Finish reading this so we can get to lunch before the end of the day."

I was embarrassed, ashamed and as humiliated as a six-year old can be. Of course, Dana could read much faster than me. I hated her for that. And I told her so, fifty years later! She had no memory of the incident. Why would she? Her world was infinitely different from mine and she was just a child too. We're actually best friends today.

Years later, I would see this first grade teacher in church. She was blind now, but she recognized my voice immediately when I said good morning. She congratulated me on becoming a teacher and probably thought somehow she had influenced that decision. She asked why I had never reached out to her professionally, as she would have been proud to mentor me.

Why would I do that? That one incident had haunted me my entire school career and I had held it against her all these years. "Oh, I don't know", I answered indifferently. With that she responded that she loved me and was proud of me. She told me that she had loved me in the first grade and she still loved me today. Who knew, and after all this time? Now that I am a teacher, I never stop children from reading just because they are a little slow. "Take your time", I tell them. "We have all day."

## Maybe if I Pray Every Night

My family held a secret, my father's alcoholism. A fact, we didn't openly face for forty years. All of this would have great impact on my life; my life's choices for some years to come. No one was allowed to see my father drinking or drunk. We were told, "Don't let anyone in the house", on those "special" times.

Once a week, the church held prayer meeting at my house and my mother was always afraid that my father would come home drunk and embarrass the family. If he came home before the meeting was over, my mother would start to shout, "Oh Jesus, oh Jesus…". That was my father's cue not to come in. He always managed, no matter what his state, to not intrude.

His alcoholism wreaked havoc with my psyche for years. I lived in fear of his freezing to death in winter, waiting for mom's prayer meeting to end. On some nights we had to go searching for him and bring him home. In the middle of the night, we would comb the neighborhood searching for him. Often he would lose precious money the family needed while in a drunken state. And sometimes I saw mommy take money from him while drunk and then lie about it later.

That behavior conflicted with our religious upbringing, but I never questioned it, or her. I never knew what triggered my father's drinking. I just knew I had to work hard to keep them both happy. Kids try to balance what is out of kilter with their parents, even though the effort is usually futile. This affected my ability to develop as a child. I couldn't be a child. I had to help maintain the sanity of my family.

No kid should have to do that. For one thing, it's not really possible to do. On sleepless nights, my mother used to tell me everything would be fine. She assured me that she got everything she needed on her "knees". If she wasn't scrubbing some lady's floor to feed us, she was praying to the Lord, as if he would appear with supper on the table.

My father stopped drinking twenty years before his death. This milestone was marked the same way as his drinking for twenty-five years was marked, with no acknowledgement.

## Nobody's Home

Usually the father is the disciplinarian in the house. Not in our family. Dad never knew what to do with us. He was rather low key in his role as father. He used to say, "Don't make me take my belt off", whenever I acted out in a public place. The worst that would happen is that he would threaten, "I'm going to tell your mother". I think he was scared of her too. We all were, as we didn't want her to be angry with us, or cry as a result of us.

Every summer we took a trip to North Carolina with mom to visit relatives. My grandmother lived on a farm. She used to make her own clothes, curtains, furniture accessories and soap. I don't know why she just didn't go to the store. She used to can vegetables and fruit too.

One time my family slaughtered a hog for dinner. I had never seen anything like that before. I never connected the dots between slaughtering hogs and a bacon sandwich. For months afterward, I could see the eyes of that hog whenever I sliced a piece of ham. Pork chops never tasted the same until the memory of that experience faded. Notice, it did not stop me from eating pork, however. Nothing, it seems, can stop my appetite for anything completely.

Nothing of that dead hog went to waste. They used every part of it. Parts were barbecued, smoked, pickled, frozen and fried. Household items were made from the skin. Even the fat was put in a large kettle and cooked for days with other "secret" ingredients to make soap. I didn't like using grandmother's soap. It was an ugly color and always smelled funny.

These trips could have been so much more educational for me, had I been mentally and emotionally ready for it. As it was, I just thought these people, my relatives, were strange. In reality, they were poor and lived a life full of ingenuity. We could use more of that; in this world of use once, and throw it away.

After years of complaining about going to North Carolina, I finally got my wish and mama left us home with daddy for those two weeks. Only, as it turns out, that wasn't what I really wanted. I really did enjoy those trips to the farm. It was another world, full of special times and special experiences I had grown to appreciate, even look forward to. Needless to say, the house was out of control while mom was gone.

Daddy had no sense of routine or discipline. No order. What a crazy two weeks, and a busy twenty-four hours getting the place in order before mama's return.

## Love is Not Enough

Our parents loved us. Aside from love, there wasn't much else they could give us. We never got real Christmas presents. I know my mother squirreled away money, but none of us would see it until after she died. This took a lot of prayer to overcome, as my life is still grounded deeply with religion. To say my mother was cheap is a gross understatement. Maybe cheap isn't even the right word to describe her, though a better word does not come to mind.

I remember one Christmas when I was nine years old. My gift was a used shaving razor and some deodorant. What does a nine year old need with either? I didn't even know what to do with it. So I got creative! I put the deodorant on my face and shaved my eyebrows off. I looked so funny I had to laugh myself, but my mother wasn't laughing. As expected, I was sent to my room and spent a lot of time in there over the holidays. What was she thinking anyway? All I wanted was a doll or a toy, something to play with.

My mother always worked on Christmas day, which I hated. She explained she would get paid time and a half, so it was supposed to be worth it. It never translated into Christmas presents for us kids. So, in a child's mind, how was it worth it? As a consequence of her working, we had usually had Christmas dinner at my Aunt Rosemary's house.

For a while, we enjoyed a warm reception, fun and games, delicious food and nice presents. Eventually, this too would become a difficult evening to endure. It's supposed to be better to give than receive during the Christmas season, but I think my extended family got tired of doing all the giving. Even when you grow up somewhat deprived, there must be more criteria for gift selection than cheap.

Growing up "cheap" was the only one I knew of. I think our relatives even stopped giving us gifts because my mother's return gifts were so, uh...pitiful, inappropriate, worthless? She could buy things you would never think to wrap as a Christmas present. It was truly amazing! She used to buy items such as a tube chap stick as a gift, for example. It got so embarrassing at church during the gift exchange that I had to stop going to the same church. I just couldn't be seen there. Everyone knew whose mom bought the toiletry items. It would have been better to bring nothing at all.

As we got older and had jobs, we instituted what we called the family auction for Christmas. Everyone would purchase four to five gifts and put them on the auction table. I would bring gift certificates from favorite stores, decorative scented candles, note cards, CDs and such. My brothers and sisters would also bring comparable gifts, usually valued under twenty dollars. Everyone had one hundred dollars of Monopoly money with which to purchase. And again, mom's items would be not just stuff you didn't really want or would never use; often they would be used, not new.

Interestingly, she always used her money to buy some of the nicest items on the table and then put them away. I'm guessing for a special occasion, or a rainy day. We were never sure if she ever enjoyed them. She had a tendency to hoard basic household items for a rainy day. Years later when I would visit, I would find twenty five tubes of toothpaste in her bathroom, maybe ten pounds of bacon in the freezer, and easily a year's supply of sugar in the kitchen cabinets. Can somebody explain that to me?

# Sandra

## If You Don't Know Me By Now

Miss Ella May Taylor was my third, fifth and sixth grade teacher. I wanted to think that she changed the grades she taught just so she could teach me again. In reality, I don't know how that happened. But, I loved her and I think she loved me too. Unfortunately, she terrified most of my friends. Their fear of her caused me some distress, as I wanted them to like her too.

Miss Taylor had been a WAC (Women's Army Corps) before she came to teach us. This previous experience would have a great impact on her, and us. She treated us like new recruits. "You need a notebook (three ring binder only), two pencils (in case one broke), and paper every day in class", she would declare. "You must come to school prepared to learn." We had inspection too. She would check our desks for the proper educational tools each morning.

She would pick up our notebooks, holding them upside down, and shake to see if any paper would fall out. If something, anything, fell out, that was the kiss of death. "Minus five points for a disorganized notebook," she would assert in cadence rhythm. She marched around the room from desk to desk checking our homework. Zero, if you didn't have it. A paddling, if it happened too many times.

I could feel her presence long before she reached my desk. The clanking heels of that approaching tall shadow, caused frightened children to flinch, even as she approached their desks. This response was mostly from the chronic abusers of the "no home-work club". I hated when that happened. It meant we all had to hear the lecture of what dim futures we would have if we lacked discipline and the simple commitment of completing a homework assignment. Miss Taylor taught, and we learned language arts, reading, writing and spelling.

Miss Taylor dressed in plain outfits that were a cross between a nun, that didn't wear a habit, and her army uniform. They reminded me of usher dresses in church. Blue, gray, and brown were her favorite colors. She wore sensible, low-heeled shoes and dark hose. I think the dark hose were to hide her thick legs. She was a thick woman and reminded me of farm equipment, stubby and hard to wear out. She frightened other people, but I knew she liked me, so I was never afraid.

She made me feel that structure was important for children. Only a certain amount of flexibility was allowed. That way "A" always equaled "B". In her ordered world, there was never any reason for conflict. She was the only woman I ever knew who never had a husband. Of course I was only nine at the time, so what did I know? In any case, in my eyes, she was non-marriageable. Just her presence was intimidating. If she scared my friends, I figured she scared men too!

I learned a lot of life's lessons from Miss Taylor. She taught me to be very clear about what I want and don't want. Speak up. Do your best. Don't waiver once you've made a decision. Though memories of her haunt me as rather rigid today, I still feel she was the best teacher I had until I entered high school. She taught us well, had great discipline, but little warmth. Young children need warmth.

When I became a teacher years later, I used some of her tactics. I'm a firm believer in the importance of keeping a notebook in class, which becomes the student's bible, so to speak. How else can you remember the important ideas and keep up with the pace of the class? I've recently left retirement and returned to teaching for only a few months, until the real teacher returns from a military leave.

Not surprisingly, Miss Ella May's techniques for successful teaching are no longer effective in the 21st century. The students I teach need a great deal of love and comforting, yet they don't trust it. I can tell by the expressions on their faces as they enter my classroom. The look says "I need a hug today. My mother didn't come home last night." As I reach out to give that hug, often times they retract with a "don't touch me" or "you gay or something?" posture. Regrettably, these students fear no adult, and reject any "sensibility" for the essential "bling bling" of their world.

# Denise

## Woman's Got Soul

She was more than a nurturing, fifth grade teacher; she was a mentor and the first to introduce me to black literature. She was Mrs. Vera Brownlee. She would teach me how to be a proud, black woman at the tender age of ten. My love of literature, cultivated by her, is still with me today, as I participate in three book clubs. As a founding member of the Evanston Chapter of Jack and Jill, a cultural, civic and educational organization for children of color, Mrs. Brownlee's influence was felt throughout the community.

One of my fondest memories of fifth grade was attending the Chicago presentation of "A Raisin in the Sun", a play about aspiring black people and dreams deferred. It was outstanding. Mrs. Brownlee went well beyond teaching the three R's. She was our protector, advocate and advisor. She told us "secrets" that no one else would, opening our eyes to the realities of the world.

As we graduated from sixth grade to junior high, she told us life would be different. For the first time, we would be attending school with white children. She armed us with knowledge that would be essential for the future. "Things might not be fair." "Things will be different," she counseled. "You will have to work harder and study longer, just to prove yourself." These truths, when prepared for, helped us to stand tall through most attempts to make us trip and fall.

Mrs. Brownlee died much too young, before she would know what we would become. She was the first person I had known, as a child, to die. This was something you just didn't experience often in childhood, except maybe with a grandparent. Even in her dying, she taught me the lesson. People close to you can die, even your mom and dad.

# Susan

## Since I Don't Have You

Growing up an only child has its disadvantages. I didn't have a brother or a sister to take the blame for anything. If something was missing or out of order, it was my fault. I hated that! Sometimes I really didn't do whatever it was that my parents were angry about. Most of the time I did and I always got caught. My dad used to hide "things that were not my business" in his special drawer. Of course that only aroused my curiosity more.

One day, I went in his drawer and stole his cigarettes. I thought that would be cool and bring prestige to me among the neighborhood children. I passed them out and we each took a disgusting puff. What I didn't know, and soon learned, was that my father would tape a single stand of hair across the seal of the drawer. If the seal was broken…you know the rest. It spelled T-R-O-U-B-L-E for me. On that occasion, my father made me smoke a cigar until I got sick. His punishment backfired though. I threw up on him.

*Mom & Dad (James and Beulah (Boots) Avery*

*Me and my parents and older brother. My sister is on the way.*

*Mother's angels*

*Me with mom and Grandma Avery on her
front porch in Evanston*

*My brother, my protector and loaner of
dimes for ice cream*

*My favorite picture with my brother, Jim*

*Me and my sister Marsha on Easter Sunday*

*Singing in the choir at New Hope Church*

*In the beginning, we were five…"*

*Aunt Carrie and Uncle John Fleming in front of their grocery store in Evanston*

*The North Shore Twelve Cotillion, July 1964*

*Taking a bow*

*My mother's sister Aunt Erma taking care
of mother's angels*

*The family visiting at Thanksgiving
in the Wisconsin home of Aunt Erma
and Uncle Leonard Jenkins*

*Picnics in Wisconsin with Aunt Erma
and Uncle Leonard*

*The family with Aunt Erma in
Wisconsin, our home away from home*

*My sister and me after a fishing trip
with Uncle Leonard*

*Me and Uncle Leonard when
we aren't fishing*

*Me with one of Diamond and
Valarie's offspring*

*Uncle Leonard skinning
a squirrel for breakfast*

*Granddad Baker in his garden
behind his home in Pueblo, Colorado*

*Family and friends in front of my
grandparents' home in Pueblo
Colorado*

*Grandma Baker, Aunt Erma, Aunt Viv, and
Mother with me and my sister outside the
cemetary in Colorado*

*My brother feeding Granddad
Baker's goats in Colorado*

Chapter Two

# Almost Grown – How Sweet It Is

*Life Is A Series Of Choices…Choose Wisely*

# Arlene

## I Wish Those Days Could Come Back Again

You think you're making choices while you live at home with your parents. You choose your friends, what party to go to on the weekend, classes to take, what to wear. That's child's play compared to the choices you make once you leave home. College is where you really start to make serious choices and then living with the consequences.

I remember my first day at Northern Illinois University, September 1964, like it was yesterday. My parents drove me and my trunk full of belongings on the 90-minute trip, west through the cornfields to DeKalb, Illinois. It was far enough to feel a sense of independence, yet, close enough to feel that a safe haven was close by, if I needed it.

I left home an inexperienced, not sure of myself, adolescent. Remnants of self-doubt were still left over from experiences with a number of those worthless teachers that I have already discussed. That would change. Thus far in my seventeen years on the planet, I had let fear and hesitation get in the way of making some really good memories. This too would change.

I had lived my childhood somewhat in the shadows of school life. I didn't have enough nerve to be the star of the production, but enough to back up the star. I was usually a part of "what's happening", but not front and center, not enough bravado. I never wanted to look like a fool or embarrass myself or my family. At least those were the excuses I told myself when I didn't want to run for student council president in grade school; decided not to run for office in the Girls' Club in high school; or try out for school plays.

I quietly worked on the school newspaper and withheld every creative idea that might have been inside of me; afraid of being crushed in criticism. I did try out for cheerleading my sophomore and junior year in high school. In retrospect, I can't imagine what gave me the courage to do so because I was really dreadful. I had the enthusiasm, the love of the team, the spirit, but little gymnastic ability. My long legs couldn't kick high enough, nor split wide enough to meet requirements.

Admittedly, my body did not possess the aptitude from which all cheerleaders are made; flexibility. At least, I came out of the background long enough to take the risk. I made a choice. My cousin Cheryl didn't succeed either, so in consolation we still had each other in the stands. We led more cheers from the stands than the real cheerleaders did from the field. If I could rewind the clock, I think I would have taken more risks and become more active in school activities, and left cheerleading to the professionals!

## Brick House...A Case for Integration

Upon arrival at Northern in the fall of 1964, we unpacked the car of all my belongings, which filled the trunk and most of the back seat of my parent's car, and delivered them to my tiny, new dorm room to be shared with my new roommate, Marge. She was from a small town south and west of Chicago.

The typical student at NIU came from small towns and suburbs in the northern half of Illinois. She was quite friendly and we liked each other right away. Her engaging smile hid the fact that she'd never met a "real black person" before, a fact she didn't reveal for some time. She carefully observed me for a whole semester. She was shedding preconceived ideas she had learned about African Americans before living with me.

That first face-to-face look must have been quite a shock. I think it was a good thing that her parents were not present at my arrival or they might have insisted on a change of rooms. We shared a lot that freshman year; fear of failure, idiot girl stuff, idiot boy stuff, cramming for exams, dorm room pranks.

We're still great friends today even though we don't see each other often. Our experience and friendship was so special that when she later married, she insisted on living in Evanston, the town where I had grown up. She and her husband have raised two beautiful girls and still live there today, some thirty plus years later. Growing up in diverse communities can have a long-term effect on solving social issues that confront us still today. If you build a strong brick house, stones can't knock it down.

## Yes We Can Can

Academically, I expected college to be more difficult. Either I was well prepared, or the real game in town is actually just getting accepted. Once invited in the "club" you have a lifetime membership. A little of both is probably true.

College is an opportunity to make the first real important choices of your life. To study or not; go to class or cut; choose a career; withstand peer pressure to spend rather than manage your money; have sex; try drugs; smoke cigarettes; and, other things. These are the decisions that could impact the rest of your life.

"You are of age now and can go to jail." This was the advice of a very wise uncle. I believe everyone should leave home and attend college outside their immediate community. How else do you discover what it takes to stand on your own two feet; live with the consequences of your decisions, behavior and actions?

At the end of that first day my parents delivered me to school, they took me to dinner at the new student union building, hugged me, waved good-bye, got in the car and left. There I stood all-alone. I wasn't even sure which way to turn and head back to the dorm! It seemed so far away at the time. What if I get lost?

I turned and started up the hill toward Lincoln Hall, my home away from home for the next two years. Each step felt laden with lead. I walked as if in slow motion into my future. I had thirty dollars in my pocket, which needed to last a month. That equates to a dollar a day for any extra expenses. There wasn't a friend in sight, even though there were two of my girlfriends from E.T.H.S who would be attending Northern freshman year. They were assigned to different housing. I had yet to run into them. It hadn't been an option to pre-select your roommate, which in hindsight, was a good thing.

I needed to be on my own, figure it out for myself without the crutch of childhood girlfriends who eventually would transfer to other universities after the first two years. It had been a long time since I'd made *new* friends. Some of my old "bike-riding buddies" were off to Washington D.C., Connecticut, Tennessee, Wisconsin and Texas. What was my plan? What would my classes be like? Who would I eat meals with? Would I ever date again? What if I run out of money? Dozens of questions circled my head like bees on a flower as I reached the top of that hill about ten minutes later. I could see on the horizon, there *she* was, Lincoln Hall, just a few more steps away. Home free. Safe and sound. At least for the night!

I recently visited my old campus and noticed that the student union was only two blocks from my dorm at the top of the hill. At the time, two blocks seemed like two miles, emotionally. It was scary being alone, on my own, exciting and oh so much fun too. I was ready to get it on; my life, that is. Four years of great, and some not so great, memories. Changes in latitude, attitude, nothing remained the same.

## Hit the Road Jack

We lived a fine existence at NIU. My friends and I studied hard and we played hard. In 1965, what we considered playing hard is poles apart from today's college kids. Our weekend started about midday on Fridays with a hot dog, basket of fries, milk shake and a rousing game of bid whist; a card game everybody played. I had to learn quickly and discovered I was a natural.

Friday night was spent at the student union. That was comparatively innocent. We bowled, danced and played cards until they shut the lights off. Lights were out about 30 minutes before curfew, which on Fridays was midnight. Every Saturday night there was a party usually given by one of the campus sororities or fraternities. Sometimes these events were theme parties where we dressed in our "suppressed desires" and danced the night away. There was no need to "hook up" as everyone danced with everyone together and separately. Remember soul train lines, the original line dance? It didn't matter who went down the line with whom. It was a partay!

Once in a while parties were held off campus at someone's apartment. Older students tended to live off campus. They were considerably more advanced socially than I was. Here's where some of the "choices" played out. To drink or not to drink; smoke or not; be late for curfew; or stay out all night. Few people did drugs in my circle of life, even though they were available if you so desired. Sex was another thing.

My mother never did find the words to explain sex to me. She basically instilled in me that "nice girls don't", so I didn't. These off campus parties brought the most dilemmas. Usually about midnight, some dude would announce, "OK, all you girls who ain't fuckin' gotta go." So, I left. The problem was making sure I had a ride back to the dorm. That was more easily achieved if I wasn't alone in my exit. At first, I expected most of the girls would be following me out the door. Most of them didn't; which in my naive, sheltered existence, surprised me. I had to learn quickly.

Curfew was one o'clock on Saturday nights and taxicabs were not an option. I usually had a plan worked out ahead of time, except plans don't always play out the way you expect. One unforgettable Saturday night, my girlfriend Sandra and I didn't make it before the doors locked. We saw the lights turn off in the lobby, as we stood there in the still of darkness. We were locked out of the dorm. It was cold and we didn't have cell phones in the sixties.

If we had knocked on the door, this would announce our tardiness, which would mean we would be on lockdown the next weekend.

We had to find a pay phone, the major means of communication before cell phones. It only took one dime for a local call. We ended up spending the night off campus on a friend's couch. Friends off campus with cars, who can pick up stranded coeds, can sometimes be a blessing too. The two of us attempted to sleep on one very uncomfortable couch.

Fully clothed, with heads at opposite ends, we held on to each other's feet, trying not to fall off. We were so apprehensive; I don't know how we ever fell asleep. We can laugh about that night today. It wasn't funny then. Survival means there must always be a plan B, as well as a backup plan to B.

## Groovin' on a Sunny Afternoon

Sunny Sunday afternoons in DeKalb were a different story. There were lots of churches within walking distance of the campus, which we preferred to the boring all denominational campus outreach services. My friends and I were fair weather churchgoers; cold was ok, except no rain please. Decked out in our fine matching shoes, purses and gloves, donned with hats tipped, we set out for a different church service to attend each week. Even our undies matched, something I can't say is true anymore. I basically go with a comfortable and clean size nine as my only necessity today. Oops, did I say nine? Don't tell! I'm working on it.

At any rate, as I recall, it was a beautiful spring day, in a sauna sort of way, and we were starting to melt under those "crowns", so we cut the usual walk short and entered one of the first churches we encountered along the path. We could hear shouting voices full of the spirit, loud tambourines and an organist full of the Holy Ghost, so we knew we had miraculously found a soulful church in the middle of the DeKalb corn fields of Illinois.

Oh, no we didn't. We walked in to find that the shouting, dancing in the aisles, gospel singing, praise the Lord church members were white folks just sounding like black Baptists on the Southside of any city in America. So there we stood, dumb founded and speechless, unable to move to a seat. The congregation looked at us like we were from another planet. The tambourines stopped and the Holy Ghost seemed to leave the sanctuary. "Every time I feel the spirit moving in my heart I will pray..." just kind of trailed off into the stained glass windows.

There he was, the white Jesus, in a life-size painting hanging behind the pulpit. At that point, no member of the congregation was thinking about *His* word. *Love thy neighbor as thyself.* Integration is fine, except it doesn't happen on Sunday morning, at least not in the sixties, not so much today either. "Uh, sorry we must be in the wrong church." We did an about-face, and didn't stop till we reached the dorm. There would be no receiving of the good word and Christian spirit that day. Amen.

## Alpha, Beta, Gamma, Delta...

I discovered there were Greeks (and I'm not talking about the country) on campus. I make the distinction because there were some freshmen who didn't know what campus Greek meant. Just making polite conversation, I once asked one of my classmates, Sasha, if she was "Greek". She proudly replied, "No, I'm Serbian" and then proceeded to explain to me the difference. I received a twenty-minute history and geography lesson. It was interesting information so I'm OK with that. We laughed later when I restated my question less ambiguously. There's nothing like clear communication.

Of the dozens of sororities and fraternities represented on campus, there was only one chapter available for students of color. There was one black fraternity, and one black sorority. The sixties were a time of change, but not major change when it came to Greek organizations. The one black sorority on campus, Alpha Kappa Alpha, was not the one I, and a few others, sought affiliation with, so we were left without a choice. My mother was a member of Delta Sigma Theta and it had always been understood that one day I also would be. It was an unwritten promise between us and of great importance to me.

After a couple of years, we started an interest group on campus campaigning for the approval of a second black sorority. This, we mistakenly presumed, would not be a major concern as new white sororities and fraternities were being established every year without issue. The University was growing, so it stood to reason that more Greek organizations would be formed as well. It would take two more years before the second black sorority, Delta Sigma Theta, was approved and recognized by the University. According to the Dean of Women, "We already had one, why did we need another?" Her name was Dean Hadnaught.

We used to say Dean Hadnaught, surely *had not*—not a brain in her head, a help in her hand, nor a loving beat in her heart. I remember entering her austere and sterile office to meet and discuss the potential for a second sorority "for us". There was nothing of a personal nature, like pictures of family or mementos of travels taken. There were no pretty collectables or pictures, just books, papers and a large desk to hide behind. She sat with her arms folded, barely giving us eye contact, as we talked. If ever there was a stereotype of a spinster, Dean Hadnaught was the living example.

I ended up pledging Delta, as did my roommate, in our respective hometowns on weekends. And then there were two of us for a whole year on campus. Finally, progress was made toward establishing an additional black sorority on campus in the next school year. By then we were seniors. Dean Hadnaught and her evil twin did not allow my roommate and me to participate in the activities of the interest group that would become the chapter of Delta Sigma Theta, the fall 1968, months after our graduation. She robbed us of what could have been a very rare experience, founding membership.

## That's the Way of the World

You don't have to accept what is. Be prepared for a potentially long, hard fight if you don't. We had to justify the *need* for two black sororities and fraternities on campus and ultimately we did prevail. A process that should have taken a semester or two, actually took years. Unpredictably to the administration, we black students didn't all think alike, have the same interests or needs. It had not occurred to them. Some of our parents had affiliated with other fraternities and sororities not present on the NIU campus at the time. It is the ultimate compliment to one's parent to pledge the same Greek organization to which they belong. In the black community, membership in Greek organizations is a lifetime commitment of service. The Greek organization and its members return as a resource; reaching back to encourage and lift up those future generations who follow. The responsibility goes beyond the college years of fun and games. This is one more thing that typical white people don't know about their black brethren.

## Someone I Would Like to Know

There was one Caucasian sorority on campus open to diversity that I became aware of. It was a local service sorority without a national affiliation, Sigma Lambda Sigma. This affiliation was to be one of my most memorable experiences in college. At the time of my membership, about five other African American women were accepted into the sisterhood; and, racial diversity was not the only difference accepted into this sisterhood. Age, culture, physical attractiveness, religious affiliation, life style and socio economic differences all coexisted harmoniously within our society.

Sig Lams, as we were called, did not have to be clones of each other to be accepted into the group. Some sororities on campus were composed of all blond, blue eyed, rich girls. Some rushed all cheerleaders. Some were all one religious affiliation. How sterile. How boring. Our group of sisters were talented, creative, gifted, open minded, open hearted and different from the mainstream. Their inclusion was based on true caring values, not the fake ones professed by so called people of faith today like the "religious right" which is neither. Sig Lam values were about helping all people in a non-judgmental way.

Instances of unwanted pregnancies; interracial dating; academic struggles; stress; pain and repressed feelings, were addressed in an environment of sincerity. Our sisters came together as a comfort and resolution to issues, not as judge and jury. This group of women represented what college life should be about; an openness to ideas, thoughts and perspectives different from one's own life experience. And we had a lot of just plain old fun too. My last two years at NIU were spent living in the Sig Lam house with a great group of women.

## Make That Move

I wouldn't trade the time I spent in college for any amount of money. College is where you make your second set of best girlfriends. They help you try new things like, for example, tampons. I won't go into the detail of how my girlfriends coached me for fifteen minutes from the other side of the bathroom door. Suffice it to say that confidence and relaxation is everything. That wondrous day, I graduated from the "bulky kid stuff". I was a new woman of the world! Becoming a woman entails a lot more than this, of course, and for me, it was a first big step. I didn't know JACK! Really.

As children growing up, my brother, sister and I were exposed minimally to the real world of sex and violence. We didn't discuss our bodies or bodily functions so readily as kids today. Youth today can experience everything virtually on daytime television, cable or any time of day on the Internet. When we were growing up, not even the married television couples like Ricky and Lucy Ricardo, or Laura and Rob Petry, slept in the same TV bed. My graduating from the "bulky kid stuff" signified a first step out of the shy, self contained, comfortable life I had been living. The power and confidence I felt transferred from this very small event to even larger ones.

I now knew material that didn't come from my mother. There was a lot she didn't advise me. It was like having a secret she hadn't the courage to share. I was a woman of the world, ready to take on almost anything, or so I thought. Could using tampons prepare me for sex? I thought maybe it would. It didn't.

## Monkey Time

Cleanliness is next to Godliness, or is it? Though we learned this lesson as children in Sunday school, we rarely witnessed it in practice within the confines of our college dorm rooms. Football and basketball games, parties, sororities, student government, and silly antics in the dorm were the activities that filled our moment in time. My roommate and I appointed ourselves the pig police on the second floor of Lincoln Hall. We would select a room or two on the floor that were particularly filthy, mainly the girls who smoked cigarettes.

Some girls were extraordinarily messy. Their closets were not utilized to store clothing, that's what the bed was for. Trash and food covered the floor, despite the fact that food and cooking were not allowed in our rooms. Though it was a fire hazard, no one adhered to this mandate. We hung food from the windows in winter as a refrigeration method. There were no portable refrigerators or microwave ovens in our day. Irons and ironing boards were handy substitutes for making grilled cheese sandwiches. Popcorn poppers were about the only cooking utensil allowed, so it was used for soup, chili and just about anything else that came in a can.

These inhabitants of the prevailing messy rooms would be the recipients of our shaving cream volcanic eruption. That's where you fill an envelope with shaving cream and seal all except one corner of the envelope. You place the open corner under the door of the chosen room and drop a heavy book on the other end of the envelope outside the door. The result is an explosion of shaving cream splattered all around the room. It was just a squirt of shaving cream, but remnants could be found from floor to ceiling. It was a mess, which usually required the inhabitants to thoroughly clean up the room.

Now this was a really fun exercise for the pig police, but not necessarily as much for the cohabitants, so most times we kept our identity a secret. It would also guarantee that when the R.A. (room advisor) did inspection, the floor would pass and we would be able to hang out on the weekend. Antics like these usually escalated during finals week. The more stress we felt, the more stupid ideas seemed to surface. Putting Vaseline Petroleum Jelly on the door-knobs and covering the toilet seats with plastic wrap were favorites. All were harmless as none resulted in injury, just a lot of laughs.

Fundamentally, all we had to do for four years was study and have fun, without getting into trouble. If you accomplished that goal reasonably well, you could live an independent life, without in reality being "responsible". An independent life is one free of parental interference, essentially on your parent's dime. Adult responsibility is something you get thrown into later, if you survive your early choices.

# Cynthia

## Can I Change My Mind...

The shelf life of a college degree gets shorter and shorter. My parents sent me to college to prepare for my life's work. I myself went to meet new people and continue my "ain't life grand" attitude, one I've had most of my life. My oldest son has that same attitude. Wonder how that happened? He just graduated from college after five years, and has started a career bearing no resemblance to his degree, and not yet providing the economic security one expects with a college degree.

College equipped me for the first eight years of my career. My first eight years were in an elementary classroom. After that I was pretty much on my own. I moved through corporate America, entrepreneurship and then circled back to the public sector. That round tripper should have provided me with more financial stability. In today's world that still eludes me and a lot of other people. His preparation may get him through two or three years. I just hope it pays his bills!

# Annie

## Lean on Me

I started a job at the phone company upon my graduation from high school. One by one, I watched my childhood friends leave for college. They really inspired me to do the same, except I didn't know where to begin. Working at the phone company gave me free access to calling all over the country, so I did. I called my friends in college and asked them, "How did you get in college?" Coming from a large family, my parents weren't able to assist me. The counselors at school did not encourage me to dream big or even develop the skills I needed to be successful in college. So though I wanted more, I was resigned to my job at the phone company. I subsisted in a low paying, entry-level job taking me nowhere, and then it happened, *a turning point in my life.*

One day as I was walking home from work, I passed by a neighbor's house. Mrs. Brownlee called me to her gate (a typical behavior in the "it takes a village" attitude neighborhood in which I grew up) to ask me how I was doing. I expressed dissatisfaction with my status at work and surprisingly she offered to help. Her husband was the president of the N.A.A.C.P. at the time. I don't know exactly what he or they did, but miraculously I was offered a new position at the phone company. This new position, which paid more money, required additional training.

Each day as I returned home, Mrs. Brownlee pulled me aside to quiz me on my performance and how the training was going. She asked where my "notes" were and what I needed to study to prepare for the next day. Notes? Study? What was she talking about? Was I back in high school? I was clueless, adrift in a boat with no paddle. Since she had been so helpful in improving my job status, I didn't want to let her or the N.A.A.C.P. down, but I wasn't sure exactly how to accomplish that feat.

This neighbor, Mrs. B. (I called her) who was not my mother or my teacher, took me in. She taught me how to take notes, how to listen for the important ideas, how to make inferences, organize and summarize. I really transformed that year after graduation, passing the test for the new position and passing a test in life. For the first time, I felt really good about me. Then Mrs. Brownlee asked me a question that would forever change my life. She asked, "Would you like to tell those people at the phone company to kiss your ass?"

I couldn't believe what I was hearing! This nice old lady talking like this to me and using the word "ass" in conversational speech! I couldn't believe my ears. More significantly, how had she come to know me better than I knew myself? What happened next was life altering. Mrs. B. called a friend at Tennessee State University and the next thing I knew, I on my way to college. Until this point some of my choices had been questionable. Listening to Mrs. B was the wisest choice I had made.

## Maybe, Maybe, Maybe

I was nineteen and off to Tennessee State University in Nashville. This was my first taste of freedom. I had not known life as living on my own, with no chores to do at home. No baby-sitting for my younger brothers and sisters. I was introduced to all kinds of new people in my life, most notably black society students from rich southern families.

I never knew they existed in this world! Black kids from farms, kids from all over the country with various backgrounds, life experiences; some similar to mine, some not, were at Tennessee State. Mrs. B. wrote letters of encouragement to me every week. I felt OK as I was armed with the knowledge that I had attended the number one high school in the country. I had attended it and, I soon discovered that it didn't mean that I had acquired all the skills necessary to succeed in college.

College was tough academically for me. Maybe if I had studied more and partied less, I wouldn't have flunked out that first year! Freedom ain't free. So after only one year, I returned home dejected and disappointed. This time I found a job at Western Union working the eight to midnight shift. It was hell. I had no one to blame but myself. My father had to pick me up every night from work as the buses didn't run that late and I couldn't afford a car. I remember thinking, life can be better than this.

Mrs. B died that year I went away to school so I didn't have her to lean on any more. I couldn't count on my mother. After all, the most she'd sent me while I was away was five dollars, which was not exactly the ringing endorsement or the financial support I needed. I thought, maybe if I tried again; maybe if I asked for a second chance; maybe if I really worked hard this time, I would succeed.

In desperation, I wrote the President of the University, who had been Mrs. B's friend and had offered me the first opportunity. I told him, if he let me come back, I would NOT fail. He must have recognized both the desperation and determination in my written voice because he did give me another chance. I went back to Tennessee State, majored in elementary education, and graduated on time. I have just retired after spending the last thirty-four years of my life teaching and inspiring other children to learn, grow and become successful adults. I'm proud of the me I have become and I know Mrs. B would be too.

# Susan

## Going in Circles

College was lonelier than I thought and full of contradictions: freedom vs. responsibility. I wanted to experience all the things my parents tried to protect me from. Yet, somehow that experience was not all I thought it would be. I tried drinking to excess, which started as fun and always ended with regret. It didn't win me the friends that I thought it would, as I mostly made a fool of myself. And, I spent too many nights on a cold floor, hanging my head over the porcelain bowl in the dorm bathroom. After which, I would have to make up some reason why I didn't return home, like studying late. I was still living at home while attending college, which left me with limited freedom, which I quickly learned still came with consequences.

Freshman year and senior year are poles apart. As I approached becoming an upperclassman, the more lonesome it got for me. It was difficult to develop long-term relationships since I didn't live in a dorm where you could really get to know other students and they in return get to know you.

Never leaving home to attend college was a big mistake! Most of my choices were still not my own. I felt like I was still in high school and that's the way my parents related to me as well. As an only child, I think the loneliness actually started at home.

If the truth be known, I had always had trouble building close relationships. I didn't venture out much and when I did I tended to overcompensate with inappropriate behavior, thus driving potential friendships away. I had to learn to relax and to not appear overly anxious.

Not having brothers and sisters at home left me learning behavior modification as an adult. If you don't have a sister at home, you need to find a friend and make her your sister. I finally did, but not until I married my husband. He had two sisters who I now claim as mine. I found my loneliness had a lot to do with me. Don't wait to start your life. It's short enough as is.

# Carla

## At Last

Going to a black college was the best thing I ever did. It was really good for me. I had grown up in a suburban environment where life and the schools were good, except there was so much more to learn about myself and people like me. Growing up, my schools were integrated, except there were very few other black children in my immediate classrooms. I was gifted, and so my teachers were obliged to place me in academically talented programs where I tended to be considered an anomaly, and treated as such. Consequently, I had few friends and lived a rather isolated childhood. I thought I was receiving, none the less, a very good education, so I accepted my circumstances. Formal education is not all that matters. It's life's education that really counts. While attending Howard University in the sixties, I learned a great deal more about life.

Many of my classmates who attended Howard University with me were from segregated communities in the South. The South, I perceived, was mostly rural, uneducated and beneath the standards I had grown up with in the North. As a student of Howard, I learned more about black professionals than I had ever thought possible. My classmates' parents were highly successful, professional people. Their communities and schools, though segregated, and perhaps because of it, were much more nurturing. When I graduated from high school that was the last I heard from my teachers. When they graduated high school, their teachers wrote letters, called, sent "care packages" and generally continued the nurturing process. Their teachers were invested in their student's successful future.

My southern counterparts displayed much more confidence and self esteem; as their all black schools had elected them student council presidents, home coming queens, council representatives, team captains, and so on. It was a competitive environment, one in which you could compete and win on a level playing field. In an integrated environment, black achievers were often seen as an irregularity, not the norm. As such, they are often marginalized, which weakens self esteem. We had to struggle to learn that whites were not inherently better. My girlfriends at Howard wore knit suits and heels to class, not jeans and sweats. These people really had "class". It was nothing like I thought.

# Denise

## Love Don't Come Easy

My four years of college were spent in an alienating environment of a mostly all white women's college on the East coast. Freshman year was the worst. There were a total of six black women on campus. Two were from Africa and one from Panama, so to me they didn't count. The cultural experiences were very different between us, even though Connecticut College for Women thought us all the same. The only thing we had in common was skin color, and even that varied.

The college administration demonstrated some of their racist's attitudes by assigning all women of color to "single" dorm rooms. We had no roommates. No roommates to learn from. No roommates to learn from us. I kept my bag packed under the bed from September to December that first year. I didn't know if I would make it! All the other white girls had chosen friends to live with. We didn't come with any friends. Coming from the same socio-economic backgrounds, these women had previously attended various private prep or boarding high schools together. Connecticut College for Women was just an extension of that life style begun in early adolescence. There was one fair complexioned "sister" on campus with very long hair who I heard had grown up in a huge, wealthy home in Washington, DC. Her father, however, was a numbers runner (which is part of an illegal gambling culture) so she was not accepted into Jack & Jill, an organization for upstanding middle-class black children. This left the sister rather conflicted as a black person. We had nothing in common, yet she was my *best* friend.

I could have lost my identity there, at that pristine white college on the East coast. Thank goodness for my upbringing in the black church. This was a place that helped to build a sense of worth for black children. No matter how badly you may have stumbled through that Easter piece, there was a "praying for you, white lace-capped" sister in the church, who hugged you anyway and told you to keep trying. Even as young adults, we were responsible for activities and programs in the church that helped us grow in life. And we were praised and recognized for our efforts. The elders taught us to read about politics and motivated us to excel intellectually.

As the politics of our country shifted in the sixties, my sophomore year changed for the better. A white classmate, whom I had met in my freshman year, asked me to be her roommate for the next semester. It was now *in* to have a black friend, so I became a novelty. I was the financially poorest member in this new group, though I had never seen myself as poor. Growing up, I had always felt privileged. My father was a professional chemist and my mother, a stay at home mom. I didn't know life was better than I had it.

Was it really better for these girls who had more material wealth than I? I found out how wild rich white girls can be. I was the virgin in the group. I was a virgin in everything; sex, drinking, partying, smoking cigarettes. I learned these things and more from my newfound friends. Contrary to the former, I also learned how to order dinner at a fancy restaurant, how to set the table for an elaborate dinner, play bridge, assimilate in "their" world, and most importantly, how to get a taxi in New York City.

Things also changed for me academically in my sophomore year. Having two English teachers, Ms. Johnson and Mr. Meredith, who were highly involved in Civil Rights activities, afforded me special attention. As English teachers, they helped me survive the writing courses, which is probably the reason I decided to major in English. Mr. Meredith even invited my parents to stay at his home when I graduated. I'm not sure to this day if he felt us too poor to afford a hotel, or if he just genuinely wanted us to stay as any friend would extend an invitation. See how racism affects your thinking and makes one question motive?

Senior year became my most memorable year. Heavy into the Civil Rights era of the sixties, we handful of black students now felt we had enough power and momentum to make demands on the administration. At that moment in time, we were twenty-five strong! It seemed like a lot of people compared to our beginnings. We demanded black studies programs, more black literature; whatever we thought would boost the recognition of our cultural heritage.

To our amazement, the Dean of the English department responded to our demands with "There is no such thing"! There is no such thing as black literature, black history, black accomplishments. It's been thirty-five years and I still hate her. I wonder if teachers realize that what they say can have a lifetime impact on students' lives. That arrow went straight through my heart.

# Linda

## Do Your Thing

They say life happens to you while you are making other plans. I kept making plans, but there was no particular reason for it other than I just couldn't make up my mind. At first, I planned to be a doctor. That was going to take too long and require too many hours of study, especially since my high school grades were average. Then I thought I would major in business. That was a good decision for one semester. There were really cute guys in the class. In fact, there were nothing but guys in the class. I was the odd ball. The professor didn't think there was much opportunity for women in the field, so he encouraged me to seek other avenues. That was so kind of him, wasn't it? He only wanted to do what was best for me, so he said.

Art sounded interesting and I was fairly good at pencil drawings. I tried art for two semesters and did well in drawing classes. I didn't do well in clay or other mediums, but I was still willing to explore the possibility. Once my father found out that I had switched to a "creative" career, he went ballistic! "I'm not spending all this money to send you to school to draw pictures that probably nobody will buy anyway." "Every artist I know is starving and has been forced to get jobs waiting tables or worse!"

Imagine waiting tables with a college degree. The conversation slipped into a .., "When I was your age…" discussion which I immediately tuned out. At this rate it was going to take five or six years to graduate and my parents were getting anxious. Goodness knows I didn't want to cut off the gravy train, so I took a serious look at the course catalog to see what major I might choose with a path to the quickest degree. General Studies was definitely out since that would leave me with wondering where to get a job upon graduation. I decided to major in Education. I asked myself, "Should that be high school or elementary?"

I chose elementary. The kids in high school are too big, physically and verbally. Then I thought what will I do if the kids ask me questions for which I have no answers? Special Education is where I need to be. Surely, retarded kids can't be smarter or quicker than me. Yep, I can handle that. I did three years of study, and just before graduation, I completed my student teaching. It was a nightmare. The students couldn't listen and sit down at the same time. My evaluation at the end said something about a lack of classroom management skills. So I did what any self-respecting girl of the sixties did in frustration. I got married and had a baby.

# Chapter Three

# Nine To Five

*How We Pay For The Stuff We Want*

# Arlene

## Tell Me What You Want To Do Babe

Essentially, I've had two careers and there's time left for a third, maybe even a fourth. My expectation when I graduated from high school was that I would have the same career, life long, with maybe two interruptions for childbirth and care. At twenty-one, I started as a Special Education teacher, even though I had always wanted to be an interior decorator and a writer. This is still under consideration. At some point I'll decide what I want to be "when I grow up".

The sixties just wasn't the time for an interior-decorating career as an African American. Remember lines like, "You can be whatever you want to be if you just work hard"? Then and now, there exists a huge gap between American rhetoric and American reality. Just ask the victims of hurricane Katrina from the 9th Ward in New Orleans. The Declaration of Independence, almost one hundred years old in the sixties, apparently was not intended for all people, especially African Americans and women. I fall into both categories.

So in 1964, my choices were to be a teacher, a nurse or a secretary. You don't have to attend college to be a secretary and personally I don't like bedpans and vomit so nursing was definitely out. I've always been interested in writing. In fact, I've fantasized becoming a famous writer, but never really thought it would or could become my reality. So I decided to teach. This turned out to be a good choice for me at the time.

## Make New Friends but Keep the Old

I met Elaine, a dear girlfriend, while student teaching. We were from different backgrounds, different schools, different cultures, and despite the differences, became instantly good friends. She grew up in the city, I in the suburbs. She attended a large University, I, a smaller one. I had a Christian upbringing while she was Jewish. And with all of that as a beginning, we "grew up" together in the profession of teaching.

Initially, we helped each other through student teaching. Student teaching was nine weeks of exposure to what one should and should not do to achieve excellence in teaching. One of my supervising teachers was so burned out and negative toward the students, that I actually counseled him out of the profession. He used to lament how poorly behaved or dumb the kids were. He would moan and complain all day. He was a really "tired" teacher, maybe even depressed. This is how I got my first job. I replaced him!

Next came the first year of real teaching. The excitement of planning for the semester, engaging the students in learning—affecting their academic and sometimes their personal lives, was both enjoyable and frightening. Could I provide all they needed? Could I captivate them and get them excited about learning? There were days I doubted myself and approached my decision to teach with a great deal of reservation. I wasn't sure if I could reach the students. It wasn't always easy to turn on that "light" of excitement to learn, that *aha* moment. As their needs were not always academic, some of the students brought complex issues to school with them that had to be addressed.

They had special needs and years of special circumstances that Elaine and I weren't always able to compensate for. Many students coming from broken homes were neglected and needy for attention, as well as academic support. Being in Special Education, our students were easily distracted. For my second period Math class, I had to remove all of my jewelry because one of my students would be fixated on the glitter and lose the entire lesson.

Special Education teachers can burn out rather quickly with all the planning and effort required. I had observed that phenomenon first hand during student teaching and was determined not to fall into that category. Some lessons I taught were one-to-one, designed based on individual needs. Others were for small and large group instruction. I spent hours after school in planning and grading papers. I never believed in busy work. If it was important enough to assign, then it was important enough to grade and provide feedback to the students.

The stack of papers on my desk grew exponentially out of control. Elaine and I were able to keep each other's candles burning. When I felt dim, she brightened me up. When she felt dim, I lent her some of my energy. We shared ideas, lessons, war stories, successes and failures. We were both dedicated to making a difference and really enjoyed our students. We worked together and socialized together and came to mutually respect each other. Our differences weren't as different as society would deem. In fact, we didn't see the distinction. We didn't let our differences become differences between us.

## Stop Look Listen To Your Heart

Elaine and I traveled through several life events together; graduate school, marriage, and children. Studying and sharing ideas for research papers was how we sometimes spent our planning periods. We taught students with special needs. We wouldn't have guessed that we would each have one to raise ourselves. You know it's a lot easier to work with other peoples' children than it is your own. With my own, I was a lot more afraid of how life would treat them. With others I learned to care, but not TOO much. When you care too much you are emotionally involved and can't make the objective decisions that would be in the student's best interest.

You certainly can't count on parents for objective decisions. I know that from personal experience now. In parents' minds, or should I say fantasies, each and every son or daughter can grow up to be president. No matter what the handicap, "they'll grow out of it." It was difficult at times to discuss recommendations for my students with their parents; what was best for them; when I knew in my heart I was often crushing the dreams they held for their children's futures. I know that disappointment too, with my own child. Because of apprehension and doubt, I was not always able make decisions that were best for her growth.

I had a tendency to be over protective and afraid for her safety. My fear was that others would take advantage of her good nature and generosity. To some extent, that has been realized. Additionally, I expected because of her inability to pay attention to detail in school, that she would never learn to drive a car, for example. She proved me wrong on this one. Today she not only has a driver's license, but gets around Chicagoland just fine except for the parking tickets and occasional illegal U-turn. She owns a car and a condo, as well.

Post high school graduation, our daughter attended a college that specialized in instruction for students with learning disabilities. This was a wonderful growth and confidence building time for her. However, like all college students, she was exposed to both the good and bad of college life. She grew academically and gained inde-pendence in her two years away from home. She traveled the East coast and experienced many adventures that would not have been possible if she had never left home. Unfortunately, the bad habits of smoking and drinking were also acquired.

Through long talks, Elaine and I shared worries we had about our special needs children. Those talks helped me get through the day, the week, the school year. We worried our kids would never grad-uate. They did. We worried they wouldn't find employment. They have. We worried they would never live independently. They do (not without a little financial help here and there). But then what parent isn't doing that today? We hoped they would find healthy and lasting friendships. We still worry about that one.

It was hard, but I had to let my daughter attempt veterinary school, even though I knew it would be too difficult for her. This was one of those times when I didn't take my own advice that would have been given to the parents of my students. To be a veterinarian had been her childhood dream; and, being just like the parents of those I used to teach, reality gave way to the fantasy. She failed and we lost a lot of money; however, she learned a lot that had nothing to do with the academics. She learned to travel independently; take care of herself thousands of miles away from her parents; make decisions; and make new friends. In short, she was able to build self-confidence. More importantly, her parents were not the ones to crush her dream. What she didn't learn, and we are still working on, is building new dreams.

## What's Goin' On?

Though it was not my first choice as a career, teaching turned out to be a good decision for me and I really enjoyed it. I like to think I did a good job, too. My students and I persevered and enjoyed much success. There were good and bad days, though. Some students were, in fact, hard to motivate. They were so damaged by previous failure that it wasn't easy trying to break through all the defense mechanisms to build on the positive. Heck, my time on the battlefield, seventeen years, was a piece of cake compared to today.

The biggest issues I had were a fight here and there, a little gum chewing, using profanity, homework not done, and now and again, a pregnancy. I once had a student threaten to throw a chair at me. His way of greeting me every morning was to refer to me as some kind of "bitch". Monday, I was a "standing on the corner bitch"; Tuesday, a "black bitch"; Wednesday, maybe a "freckle face bitch", "stupid bitch" and so forth. Just add any adjective in front of "bitch" and I was it any given day of the week

Until one day, I preempted him with "Good morning Henry, and what kind of bitch am I today?" From that moment on, he ended the practice. I'm not sure why. Sometimes our ingenious behavior management techniques just happened to work accidentally!

I once taught a fourteen year-old pregnant student who, because she had used birth control, confided in me that she didn't know why she got pregnant. When questioned as to which method of birth control she used, she replied, "Contraceptive jelly." I asked her what she did with it. To which she answered, "I put it on my toast every day!"

I wanted to laugh, except it was more important to seize the educable moment. This was sad, so sad. Was this teaching and learning, or had "sense" left the building? Discussing birth control was not acceptable curriculum at the time, but somebody had to tell the poor girl the truth! I could write another whole book of such stories. For years I was the best party entertainment among my friends. All I had to do was share the day-to-day stories about "my kids".

And today, "they" still say we shouldn't teach birth control in school. THEY DON'T KNOW JACK! This is especially true of the guy in the classroom next door who sits and reads the newspaper all day while the students run wild. Or the guy down the hall who has been using the same ditto worksheets so long they have yellowed with age.

## Midnight Train to Georgia

It's easy to see what's wrong but harder to change it. Three years of my teaching experience were spent in the Cobb County public schools of Georgia. I taught high school English Literature, American History and Physical Science to students with learning disabilities. Some of my students were from poor and rural areas, which at first blush I thought was different, but experience eventually taught me, was not so different from the inner city students I had taught.

These students weren't chewing gum but tobacco. I had to closely check their cheeks before entering the classroom daily. Gee, that was fun. They didn't have handguns, but shot guns in the back of their pick up trucks, which was not illegal by the way.

In time I began to notice that some of my female students were enduring what I would consider abuse from some of their boyfriends. The boys would verbally boss them around, demand service without complaint, and generally disrespect what the girls had to say, or might want to do. I expected the girls to stand up for themselves and exert their feminine power, instead of cowering under pressure to "obey".

Often I would take them aside and offer advice for speaking up, even breaking up if necessary, to preserve self pride. At times before I could begin my lessons for the day, I would have to listen to their issues, which would only lead to distraction if I did not give them time for expression. What I discovered was this redneck culture was quite chauvinist.

One of my students was having trouble getting his girlfriend to "shut up" when told. This was a routine expectation among my male students. Their women were expected to do as told. At any rate, it was really beginning to annoy this boy as she tried to prevent him from doing what she considered, and I agreed, were destructive behaviors such as drinking beer and driving fast. That was drinking and driving at the same time. I thought this to be a considerate action on the part of the girlfriend.

He thought her behavior an intrusion on his manhood of fifteen years. He intimated to me that he had been advised by the girl-friend's father to spit tobacco in her mouth if she gave him too much lip. "That's what I do to her mama when she won't shut up." Ugh! My advice was getting the girls in more trouble than I expected and could result in physical abuse. This was both depressing and frustrating for me. The impact of the cycle of poverty and igno-rance is the same whether urban or rural. And I'm trying to teach these kids English Literature, American History and Physical Science? I felt like the Lone Ranger.

## Tossing and Turning

At thirty-two, I was working in a part time educational consulting job. My kids were young and I was trying to do the "super mom thing" —work, go to graduate school and take care of their needs too. It seemed to work out fairly well as my husband was pretty good at sharing responsibilities at home. My part-time job was two to three days a week with mini contractual obligations, which for the first time in my life, afforded me flexibility and freedom during the workweek.

This I found worked well for my psyche. I was working as a consultant helping teachers in schools with special needs clients. I really loved this job. It allowed me to experiment with new ideas, provide expertise and the opportunity to grow and learn as well. What I didn't know, I had to learn quickly, as you will see in the story below.

Often times, in this "consulting" job, I found myself in the position of being the *authority* on many different educational topics such as behavior modification, lesson planning and various instructional strategies. I had to provide in-service sessions for teachers, some of whom were not certified teachers.

At one facility, they were having a problem with the clients, retarded adults, who were expressing rather aggressive sexual behavior. Some were expressing public displays of affection (i.e., kissing and more), while others were openly masturbating during "nap time". Now, why adults needed a nap period, which closely resembled preschool naps, is beyond me. It was my job to formulate strategies to curb if not eliminate this behavior altogether.

I can speak for hours on reading and Math instructional strategies off the top of my head. On this topic, I was clueless. Retarded adults have the same "feelings" as every other adult, but lack the intellectual ability to understand and control the actions associated with those feelings. This makes them vulnerable as well as problematic to the public. Fortunately, I had a week between in-service sessions. I spent hours in research to prepare myself for each in-service, basically staying just a step ahead of the questions the teachers were asking during my seminars.

Needless to say, the first thing to go was "nap time". This did not go over well with the teaching staff, who were disappointed to lose break time; however, it certainly did reduce the number of masturbation episodes. We also did a lot of role-playing of what was appropriate public behavior. Now that could have been a made for TV comedy episode.

The sixties were a modest time when most people didn't discuss sex openly and publicly. And here we were, my colleague Carlos and I, "modeling" appropriate and inappropriate sexual behavior and language. For example, we had to teach them to use real terms, like penis, instead of weenie, dick, shaft, Johnson and a host of other descriptors. After modeling, everyone had to practice. Practice makes perfect they say.

## Livin' for the Weekend

I've just retired from my second career in sales with a large corporation. This career was unexpected. I thought you had to be really smart to work for a big technology company and never expected to be hired. Surprisingly, and probably because I had experience in the education field, I was offered a position to work with the sales team calling on K-12 schools and clients. I took the job and felt really insecure and inexperienced at first. My subconscious was giving me negative input, casting doubts on my ability.

The training program was extremely difficult. After months of study and pretests in the branch office, we traveled to another city for four consecutive weeks of classroom instruction. On the first day everyone had to take a test. If you didn't pass, you were sent back home to the branch office in shame that very afternoon. I spent a lot of time studying while my much younger classmates were partying late into the night. That was not weekends, but every night. We had tests almost every day and new information was provided in a fire hose instructional method.

The hose would open at eight o'clock in the morning and turn off around six in the evening. It was up to the individual student to drink as much as possible. My hard work paid off. I did well on my tests and ultimately landed the second place position in my sales class, which was an additional two weeks, once basic training was successfully completed. Frankly, I think I should have been first, but then that's another discussion. I rang the big bell (signifying a perfect sales call) four times during the two weeks of sales school, more than anyone else in my class.

We used to refer to the retired men who did the customer call role-play with us as the terminator and the shredder. Some rookies left their practice calls with these two in tears. They were tougher than any real customer I've since encountered. For years, after returning back to the branch office, I wondered what I had been afraid of. I guess I was afraid of failure. I was out of my element, teaching kids I knew. The customer environment I was to cover, I knew very well. The difference between a 3641 and a bus and tag cable, was something that I didn't know Jack about.

In training school, I had to learn it all. It was an alphabet soup of acronyms that only a "beautiful mind" could sort out. It was like de ja vu in biology class again. I wasn't expected to succeed. Once again I managed to conquer the challenge.

I returned to the office after the six weeks of training a different person, trying to live up to the perfect image. I played the expected game, wore the uniform of a tailored power suit with feminine bow tie and white blouse, complete with navy pumps. I worked the long hours and even took work home. My husband and I took shorter and shorter vacations that were more like extended weekends than the two weeks that usually define a real vacation.

As I began meeting and working beside my colleagues, I realized there wasn't much to fear. Some of them didn't know JACK either! I was afraid of not measuring up and soon discovered that my expectations for myself were higher than those held by most of my co-workers. These people were not larger than life after all. They were not superior to me. I used to watch them from my desk in our high-rise building over looking the Chicago River. We didn't have private offices, just a desk and a file cabinet among a sea of desks in an open bay.

I watched them every morning as they crossed the bridge. A parade of stiff necked, blue suits with their Starbucks cups in hand. I don't know what I was worried about! I told my subconscious to go to hell and to never let me down like that again.

## Hello Stranger

My job was to sell computers, instructional software and services in the K-12 Education industry. Initially this was like selling myself, first, to total strangers. People buy from people they like and trust, we were told. Product content, of course, was a perfect match for me with my educational background. I thought I could truly make a difference so I was psyched. The Education Industry falls into the Public Sector sales division, which includes education, government and health care.

Public Sector accounts are tough, as they tend to have strained budgets and lots of bureaucracy. In their world there is no sense of urgency. In my world, I was expected to meet quota expectations every quarter and there was a constant sense of urgency. Three months seems more like three weeks when you've spent hours sitting outside CIO's (Chief Information Officer) offices waiting for appointments that took five to six requests and several weeks to get, only to be rescheduled because "something came up".

The sales cycle was long and the clients were generally slow to change from doing things the way they've always been done. I observed teachers still using instructional techniques that their teachers used twenty years prior. Then they wondered why the children who bear little resemblance to children of yesteryear were not motivated or responsive to their attempts.

Often there was no pressure for change from the administration until incredibly bad news had been publicly exposed in the newspapers. Then they wanted everything done by yesterday, but just until things quieted down again.

The customer is always right, and nothing is ever the customer's fault. I learned this message early, even though it wasn't true. I would be asked to provide a statement of work (SOW) for agreed upon services to be provided. These were documents that were put in place to clearly define expectations, expectations for the vendor and expectations for the customer. It never failed to happen that customers would want to change direction once work has begun.

Now this is fine, but it can often times materially affect the contract, requiring more resources and/or money. Even though the customer requested the change, it was rare that they would want to pay for it. They would ask for changes in scope that we, as the vendor, would often do in good faith in an effort to build the relationship. Remember, people buy from people they like and trust, so we try to keep them happy.

One particular customer in my patch routinely asked for changes in scope which my company did for no charge, foolishly thinking we were enhancing the "partnership". At the end of the project, of course, the finished product was not the same as what was stated in the SOW. Now, per guidelines, we attempted along the way to secure a customer signature for the agreed to changes that were done at no additional cost. We never got the signature and we didn't get paid for some of the work as completed either.

Ultimately, end users complained that the solution was not exactly what they expected either; as the changes were not appropriately communicated to them by their administration. Of course, you know who was blamed. We were. No good deed goes unpunished!

## Twist and Shout

In the beginning of the use of technology in the classrooms of America, my customers were not especially good at differentiating between Intel PCs. There were Apples and there were PCs as far as they were concerned. With their view being fairly simplistic, a PC was a PC. We competitors in the PC space, however, differentiated ourselves by service, reliability and support. To us, the differences were major. I sold many a computer based on these three values.

On one particular day, I received an irate call from a customer whose name was not particularly familiar to me, so I listened attentively. I prided myself on personally knowing my customers as I had visited them on many occasions and wondered why the lady's name was not ringing a bell with me. This was a client that I had inherited because another sales rep had left the business, so perhaps she had fallen through the cracks.

Ms. Kathryn, the lab teacher at this small school district, proceeded to scream and shout about how unreliable my product was. "The systems are down every other day. You sold us junk, garbage. I can't teach like this. You better get out here or else..." I took these complaints seriously as one unhappy customer calls another, who calls another, and it can be over for future sales. I was also measured on customer satisfaction, so I dropped everything I was doing and drove the ninety minutes to her school.

When I arrived, Ms. Kathryn continued the ranting and raving for another fifteen minutes as she showed me around her lab. I listened and looked and finally I had to ask her. "Where are the PCs that you bought from my company?" I didn't see any of my product in the room. "You're looking at 'em," she said. Except, they weren't mine. They were what we used to refer to as clones or white boxes, not a brand name in the industry. Though red faced, Ms. Kathryn never apologized for her error. She simply turned on a dime and said as she exited stage left, "Well, they're all the same." I left without comment. What was left to say?

## Shop Around

My customers wanted everything practically for free, too. No price seemed low enough no matter what value you brought. Some customers used to ask me what they'd get if they bought my products. Since I had worked for days on my professional presentation, I felt prepared to answer this question. I attempted to express the value of my products and services versus the competition, except what I think what they really wanted to hear was a "free trip to Vegas or Mexico".

Some of my competitors did take customers on free, lavish "educational" trips. We never did. Eventually, I just told them they get ME. That's the difference. I'm the difference. I'm committed to your satisfaction and success with my products. Surprisingly that worked most of the time. Go figure. Case in point, I used to unpack boxes of PCs when they shipped to my schools; helped to inventory, install and sometimes attended training sessions to lend a helping hand. The principals, for the most part, appreciated that I was willing to get "dirty" with them.

Training sessions proved fascinating as well as part of the implementation of my job. It was important for future sales that I had successful implementations which meant training was key. This was usually a released day or two for teachers to learn the software program and strategies for effectively integrating technology into their daily lessons. That was a lot of material to cover in one to two days. Teachers were used to a two thirty or three o'clock end to their day, and our training classes routinely ended at four o'clock in the afternoon.

On more than one occasion, when the clock struck three, one or more teachers would stand up and announce "time to go!" and then leave the class. It would remind you of a coo coo clock, "coo coo, time to go, coo coo, time to go!" It was shocking and embarrassing to the other professionals in the class and to the instructor trying to lead the class. Sometimes teachers make very poor students. At other times, I worked with wonderful clients who were

*137*

dedicated to the cause and understood working together for the achievement of all students.

We persevered for years making a difference, providing successful teaching and learning solutions for students. I used to visit these locations frequently to remind myself why I continued to do this job despite the headaches and disappointments. I always left reenergized, ready to lead the charge again.

## Chasing Rainbows

Unless you are one of the very lucky few for whom work is "play" (i.e. athletes, actors, golf and tennis instructors), accept the fact that at times, most times, your job is torture. I know, because I've been there. I've had customers that seem to enjoy being miserable. No matter what I tried to do for them, they were still unhappy. I think it had more to do with their own job satisfaction than anything my company brought to the table.

I've had managers who expected more each year though they offered fewer resources to support my efforts. This expectation accompanies the proverbial "spin" that the new process or new way of doing business is better for you and improves service to the customer. And castor oil tastes good too! Ever notice how the prices of products go down but your sales quota never does? If I was fortunate and had a really great sales year, my reward was an even higher quota for the next year. I had set my own new baseline. That was really smart of me!

There were times I really felt like telling my employer to do like the song says and *take this job and shove it*. Except, my husband and I had a mortgage and two mouths at home to feed. So you read the memo and weep. Our jobs paid for most of the things in life that we enjoyed. So, I had to deal with it and get on with life as part of accepting my adulthood. I was following a career path with no planned for, or expected ending. I continued marching through each year, attempting to make my quota with a sales plan I rarely understood. Make the number and I'll make the money was my mantra. That didn't always happen either.

Additionally, I was expected to put a development plan in place each year to chart a desired career path, except I didn't know what I wanted to do long term, much less how I should get there. At one time I considered marketing as a potential future and attempted to take several online courses in preparation for the week-long, teacher led classes. The problem was these classes interfered with the day-to-day requirements of my current sales job, and management was unsympathetic to my plight.

Theoretically, they are supposed to be supportive of your career objectives. Any dreams I had of management or other areas of interest were ignored or not encouraged as "out of my reach" at my age. It felt like high school all over again. It's easy to dream and much harder to implement the dream.

## No Where to Run, No Where to Hide

Sometimes good just ain't good enough. A good rule of thumb is to learn something new everyday no matter what your job. If the corporate experience has taught me anything, it is to be prepared for change. Change was the only constant. So in an effort to meet that challenge, I endeavored to keep my skills up-to-date and adjust as the environment or management transformed; I tried to exceed expectations. I struggled to not just read the writing on the wall but to anticipate what would be written. That requires genius and mostly luck. I kept my skills updated, checked out the company website to keep abreast of new offerings and directions of the business.

I was victorious much of the time. At least that was my perception. I watched as others were downsized from the business. They had not seen the handwriting on the wall, I said to myself, and made preparations. My team, once comprised of about five sales representatives and five system engineers, dwindled to just me in just a few short years. Once again, the Lone Ranger. My customers, often difficult to deal with, didn't pay their bills on time, or not at all. Who would want that headache? Surely this would insulate me against job extinction as I assumed no one else would want my job. I was secure! I thought.

I adjusted to new managers, one after another. Training new managers year after year can become exhausting, as well. With few exceptions, they all started out thinking either I didn't know my job or should have to prove myself. I had to establish my worth and verify my value again and again. They often wanted to accompany me on calls, to observe my ability to articulate the company offerings, close a sale and scrutinize my paperwork. Ultimately, they were always pleasantly surprised. Why is that? This is especially true of white supervisors over black employees. If I were that incompetent, how could I have graduated college and become employed by this prestigious company?

These managers didn't exactly think that I was brainless, but somehow they couldn't assume me to be qualified either. Then just when I've made a believer out of them, they're off to the next job, whether ready or not, forgetting about my promotion and my deserved raise and leaving me to start the *breaking in* process over again with a new manager. Though I didn't recognize it at the time, my job security was just as fragile as my work relationship with each of them.

In holding the all-important, client-facing job, I continued to earn several recognition awards and one hundred percent clubs. I assumed I had job security. There was safety in success. But you know what? Companies can still make you disappear when their plans and commitments change. And they do, every quarter. I was in the right place, must have been the wrong time.

## Here's a Quarter (Call Some One Who Cares)

At some point I had to ask myself, "What happened to my career?" I worked hard, stayed late, gave 'em all I had. I played by all the rules, and discovered management could still "erase" me despite being a consistent contributor to the team. That must be what qualifies them for the big bucks. Hard work does not always equal victory. I always thought one should have to accomplish something before you could be proud of yourself. I think I have and I was.

I was not one of those people that begin each Monday looking forward to Friday, counting the days until the next holiday. I put my heart and soul into trying to make a difference. In corporate America, some of us have to work a great deal harder than others, yet I was optimistic and not angry about that reality. Some of us are never recognized for our creativity and leadership, while others seem to receive reward after reward just because—just because they speak well, just because they look good, they're male, the right race, know someone, have the right connections, live in the "right" neighborhood, drink together, play golf or, just because.

Eventually, I learned that hard work doesn't always pay off. But it pays off better than not working hard. I have a quarter and am still looking for the someone who cares.

## If it Ain't One Thing, it's Another...

"Arlene, this isn't about performance. I'm over head count and I've decided to cover your customer with a part-time rep, instead of a full-time one." I didn't see it coming, the day my manager informed me that I had sixty days to find another job in the company or take a package. Well, I did and I didn't. In one way, I was more fortunate than others in my situation. Most employees were given thirty days. Finding jobs before had never been a problem, so I expected it would again be true for me.

My resume opened any door on which I knocked. Take a package? Never. I was insulted! Didn't my manager recognize and value the skills I brought to the team, the work effort displayed on a daily basis? What about the prospects I had uncovered? Big opportunities were about to unfold. You need me, I said. To my surprise, the network I assumed would be of support to me, didn't materialize either. Colleagues wished me well, offered a few suggestions and sympathy. They weren't able to provide the help I really needed. In all probability, they were ducking the same silver bullet that finally hit me. Ultimately, it wasn't about me.

It was about what was best for the company, as some bean counter who is making the decisions in corporate headquarters, sees it. It's always about survival of the company and stock options. So even good people can be terminated, like me. Like you. We live in a world called "high performance" selling. Translation: the company can fire you even if you are an excellent and successful employee "just because". You are an expense and they need to come down in head count. Just because you only made your quota while others exceeded quota. Just because your skills are in one area and the business has decided to move in another direction. Just because you have the job that a dear friend of the boss wants. Just because you are a minority and perceived to add "less value". Just because the business no longer wants a full time investment in your customer set. So there you go!

Historically, in hard economic times, remaining jobs are reserved mainly for white males. This is never verbally expressed directly. It is when you start to hear things like, "He got here through affirmative action." "These minorities are getting jobs/scholarships that I'm more qualified for." "They don't really want to work anyway." "Women don't need to work." "They should stay home with the children." From my own experience, I have noticed when downsizing occurs, all things being equal, African Americans and women seem to go first.

Generally, the white males, who have the decision-making authority, often have a personal relationship with the other white males on the team. So regardless of skills or resources needed, the tendency is to make the decision in favor of the one you like, the one most like you, the one you owe, the one who helped you. That's just the way it is. So you see, sometimes no matter how well you prepare, you still don't see that brick wall coming. Sometimes you see it coming and your "breaks" quit working. Another affirmation that I didn't know JACK. JACK can be disguised in many forms!

## Looking for Success in all the Wrong Places

People of color, especially African Americans, are often overlooked for promotions, assignments, opportunities, because it is assumed they have an inferior education or were hired because of affirmative action. In reality, affirmative action is needed to level the playing field for just that reason. My husband worked over thirty years with a large Fortune 500 company. He is a very intelligent and creative person whose talents were largely overlooked or under recognized during his tenure with the company.

Because he attended college on a basketball scholarship, it was inappropriately assumed that he was accepted based on athletic ability, and then probably hired through the dreaded, so-called unnecessary affirmative action policy. The truth is, he was offered dozens of academic scholarships, as well as athletic ones upon his graduation from high school. He chose to attend and graduated from Northwestern University, hardly considered an "athletic" school.

This black man displayed marketing, as well as, technical prowess throughout his career and achieved some degree of accomplishment by his selection to various managerial positions. He was often the "go to" person for ideas and to get the job done by both his African American peers as well as Caucasian ones.

However, the promotions were harder to come by and the glass ceiling was all too easy to reach in a very short time. This born achiever pretty much made his own deals happen. There was no mentor, no greased path, no one really looking out for his career or future. He did well despite the lack of recognition and under-utilization of his skills. However, the company failed to gain access to the full depth and breadth of what he had to offer.

Their loss. This bright employee had to look elsewhere to fulfill those talents and skills. He utilized that brainpower to build an airplane in his garage! How many other talented minority men and women, ignored at work, are home "building airplanes"? In this global economy of stiff competition, America cannot afford to throw away bright and talented people based on ill-conceived fears and prejudices.

## Rescue Me

Never fail to try again and again. For six weeks, after being downsized, I sought help and advice from others to find a job for me. Then it hit me! I had to rescue myself. It was time to elevate my game. I decided to pitch my value to higher-level management who understood the "big picture". That meant he could think beyond one quarter of the year. I managed to save myself in the ninth hour and acquired an even better job, one that allowed me to potentially make a bigger difference in my industry.

This job allowed me to elevate my skills on a larger playing field. Of course, it didn't hurt that this executive was also black and "understood" the way things are in large American corporations. Nevertheless, it is still important to learn the rules, in case you ever need to bend them a little or go for broke and break them. Rules can be broken, if done properly.

I had previously pitched my case to my manager and his manager, however I didn't get the attention that was needed until I went several levels above them. This I don't recommend unless you have no other options and nothing to lose. For me there was nothing to lose. It's a game. The game requires you to invest yourself and invest in yourself. You can't get tired or too comfortable. You also can't play the game alone, so be sure to network with those around and above you. And, be sure to mentor those who come behind you. They have no clue how the rules of the game can change. And JACK's not telling anybody anything.

## This is a Man's World

So, here I am. I've survived one downsizing and have a new job in a new division, with new people whom I have to convince of my value. This is not easy to do for several reasons. One, my manager, fairly new to the company and his position, thinks he needs to micro manage his direct reports, no matter how much experience we may bring to the table. He now requires a mountain of paperwork to detail weekly activities and goals. I suffer from his lack of confidence in me, which is more the result of his DNA, than mine.

He starts our relationship with an assumption that I'm not as good at my job as *the others*. *The others* are more like him, that being white and male. He has already in the first two months of the job "retired" the only other person of color on the team. So that just leaves me left to sweep out of the door with the next house cleaning. The next new requirement is that he must attend three customer calls a quarter with me.

I continue to fight allowing his lack of confidence in me, to transfer into my psyche. Eventually, we make the call together and it doesn't just go fine, it goes just great. He's pleasantly surprised. Rather than pleased with his response, I'm annoyed that I had to prove myself yet again while *the others* go about their business, whether they have any or not.

My job is business development, which means I pursue daily business opportunities with new and previous customers. Just when I think I have finally earned respect from *the others* in this new department, they once again remind me of the real deal. These would be the members of the same group of *others* who often share little or no personal involvement in closing business, but are always the announcers of the contract signings on internal pipeline calls.

On one occasion, after weeks and months of developing a relationship at a university in my territory, I have uncovered a prospect. I telephone one of *the others* to make a call on the customer with me to continue the qualification process for this new potential opportunity. He is a pretty good guy to work with. Even though by birth he has membership in the club as *the others*, he is in agreement with me, that the opportunity is viable.

Upon return to the office and engaging in the usual follow-up activities, conference calls and emails to internal resources related to this opportunity, the guy is chastised for making the call with me. He is told the call should have been made with another member of our so-called team instead of with me. The assumption is that he took me on the call and not the other way around. This was a wrong assumption, and typical. Next he is instructed to never make one of these calls again without the knowledge and approval of one of *the others* who is a specialist in the available solutions that *the others* own. Once again, the assumption is that I don't know Jack.

So, fine, I have identified the opportunity and will turn it over to one of *the special others* for their follow up. This will allow me to continue pursuit of additional opportunities, knowing that this base is covered. The customer, however, not knowing the rules of engagement, continues to communicate with me. I pass along these communiqués to *the others*. When *the others* get through posturing and tossing the ball around, guess where it lands? That's right, back on my plate to close. I love it. Sometimes you just have to play the hand you're dealt. You can still be a winner and keep an eye on *the others*.

## Signed, Sealed, Delivered

So, I lasted another two years in this new position and that was my game plan. I needed another two years to enhance my retirement plan. Exactly two years, two weeks later, the news came again. "Arlene, the company is divesting in the central region where business has been slow. It has nothing to do with your skills and work ethic you see..." My manager, whom I thought would have delivered that message with delight months earlier, actually seemed sincerely distressed to deliver the message now, after getting to "know" me better. This time, the handwriting on the wall was quite visible. It came as no surprise. I could have written the message on the wall, myself.

In truth, I was looking forward to the opportunity to start my third career life. I had spent the last three quarters of 2005 with buzzard's luck anyway, that being, can't kill nothin' and won't nothin' die. So give me the check, boys, and I'll be on my way.

Fortunately, at the time I separated from this company, I was eligible for retirement. However, there would be no celebration, despite the fact that I had given eighteen years of my life. That's long by today's standards. There would be no hosted dinner, no words of appreciation, no thank you, no letter, not even an email and no obligatory watch. Not even a drink after work. Just, "Your paper-work is in the mail and call the eight hundred number for the employees' service center. They can answer any questions and set everything up for you."

I'm thinking thanks, thanks a lot, for nothing, zilch, zero. I devoted my last eighteen years to their service; and it wasn't good enough for any sort of recognition at occasion of my retirement that I had ever existed.

You have to last thirty years for that. At thirty years, that recognition would include a book of letters from your colleagues, if they take the time to write them, a small gift chosen from a catalog of several choices, and dinner for you and nine guests. Actually, that's what you get for surviving twenty-five years. I've never attended a retirement dinner nor known anyone to have one, so maybe all you get when you retire with fewer years is the book of letters.

I'm five months into retirement and still waiting to see what may happen; probably nothing unless I personally initiate it, which I did. Eventually, I received a book of letters from a few colleagues and a small gift chosen from a catalog of less than a dozen choices. What was there to miss? It makes me glad to be gone. Exactly one year after I departed, so did my manager. What goes around....

## Give Me the Beat Boys

Understanding the *code* is critical. To be successful today, black Americans still need to be able to decode the political rhetoric of white Americans. Unfortunately, racism is still the underpinning of most decisions made in this country. It is pervasive in all we do, yet still denied or forever hidden, from white folk's reality it seems. Politics appear to have irreversibly polarized this nation based on hidden and denied racial agendas. There are code words used to hide the real agenda.

Like NBC (no black content), or we need more green space (which means build a park instead of subdivisions because too many blacks are moving in). School vouchers are really a way for white America to get money back from the public school system to help finance their private school desires. Vouchers are touted as a means for minority students to have access to better schools, except in reality, the students from these communities are not likely going to be accepted at the school of their choice, regardless of a voucher. The additional financial burden plus transportation issues also make this option highly unlikely for poor and minority students.

"No Child Left Behind" legislation under the Bush administration on the surface sounds admirable. The actual implementation, which is under-funded by the federal government in reality, leaves a great number of children behind. It is imperative not to be fooled by the rhetoric.

Diversity, another code word, is a term often used to replace the dreaded "affirmative action". Many like to use this word as an inflammatory technique to imply racial quotas. Affirmative Action was designed to level the playing ground for minorities who have been discriminated against for generations. It does not require quotas.

In effect, the results of diversity efforts actually water down African American participation by including every other minority group; women, gays and the disabled. Yet schools and businesses will report their diversity numbers and efforts in a positive light when in actuality, the numbers for African Americans are significantly down. The new code word for diversity is now "constituent customer sets". We're getting more and more generic to hide the true meaning of what is being communicated.

In the 2000 presidential election, George Bush, the Republican candidate, kept referring to "compassionate conservatism". Here's a code word with no real meaning. There's no such thing! It just sounds like a positive goal. It's designed to keep party moderates comfortable and on board. Typical neo-Republicans pretend with rhetoric that they are not racists, but if one looks at history, it's obvious that the people who lead their party today are made up of "Dixiecrats". These would be the same people who left the Democratic Party in the sixties just after the Democrats embraced minority participation.

That old Southern block is still alive and well. And not just in the South. I recommend that if you can't win them all, aim high anyway. If you lose don't lose the lesson. Invest in yourself. Never give up. Never quit. Correct your mistakes. And never let 'em see you cry. By all means, learn the code.

## For the Love of Money

Even more than race, it's about money. This brings to mind another code word, "frame". How should we "frame" the message to *the people?* Politicians are good at framing messages. Republicans are especially adept at "framing" information, which in actuality is disinformation. For example, when justifying, the year 2000 tax breaks on inheritance for the wealthy, they discussed at length how not providing the tax break would hurt the family-owned farms.

Now no farms had been lost due to taxes in this way, however, they were able to make average people think this tax policy was some how beneficial to them. It was not. Another example is referring the need to strengthen social security. Their idea of strengthening social security is actually destroying the program as we know it. This was an additional way to further divide the country. This time it's not black and white, gay vs. straight, born again Christians vs. other religions, but young vs. old. The argument is that young people, of whom there could potentially be fewer in the workplace, will bear the burden of supporting a large number of retired baby boomer generation seniors.

The real issue is the government attempting once again to provide tax breaks to corporations by reducing the amount they would be paying into social security. This is already happening through the exportation of American jobs overseas. When politicians "frame" information, they are actually misrepresenting the real deal. In other words, they are lying. These are called wedge issues. It's about money. As has been advised, one should *follow the Benjamins*. Those that have it want to keep it ALL. Even our elected officials, who are supposed to represent their electorate, are influenced and distracted by personal benefits and favors they receive by corporation lobbyists.

## Don't Let Money Rule You

Somewhere, around forty something, we start to define *real success*, which I figured out is about things more essential than money; if you're not a right wing Republican that is. Since the kids were older now, I thought it was time to get more focused on the career again. So, at forty, I started that new career as a sales representative in corporate America. I was able to use my years of experience in education in my new job, as my territory and sales industry was education.

It was really fun, at first. I had the opportunity to impact the education of a greater number of students than just the thirty or so I had in my classroom as a teacher. In the Midwest, schools were unable to revolutionize instruction, especially with the tight budgets they were forced to endure. Consequently, I've had frustrating years and some good years.

Still, I envisioned grand goals and had high ideals for making a difference. I imagined one day the headlines in the *Chicago Tribune* would read "Chicago Public Elementary School Children All Reading on Grade Level." Of course, this would be as a result of the courseware products and the training provided by my company. What I didn't know was how hard it would be to change the way things were. My company's products and methodologies required teachers to change the way they were teaching. If you do things the way you've always done them, you will get what you've always got. And lately that wasn't so great.

My customers were stuck in a "this is how we've always done it" mode of operation. Here and there, I encountered more innovative principals, who encouraged risk taking among their teaching staff and embraced change. I loved visiting these success stories as a way of motivating me to continue the journey.

I always believed in the products I was selling, so it was exasperating when I was unable to close a sale. In fact, I could be personally insulted if customers didn't buy. I wouldn't be out there pitching them if I didn't trust in my product. I believed that customers could actually get results and thus, expected a sale everywhere I went. A real salesman doesn't take anything personally. The difference between me and a real sales person is that they can sell anything. I can't. I have to like it myself, believe in it myself. It's not supposed to be personal, but for me it was. I learned that later, except it still didn't change my behavior much. I just know the difference and accept it.

I didn't make a fortune selling in Education industry. More importantly, most of the time, I felt good about what I was trying to accomplish. I have to make a difference wherever I go, or at least try. So, it is, to me, incredibly more satisfying to make a difference in the lives and education of children than it is selling to banks or companies like Enron. Someone once told me, when you leave a place, *they* should know that you have been there. I always hoped that when I have left a job, a place, a relationship, that I would be remembered for an unparalleled legacy.

Don't get me wrong; I do enjoy the things that money can buy. Rich is definitely better than poor. I keep a healthy attitude and balance and don't go off the deep end in either direction. I've tried to keep both oars in the water and use them wisely, rowing in the right direction.

## Tell Me Why

Tell me why religious people preach "love thy neighbor" yet live in segregated neighborhoods? The very people who marched for Civil Rights in the sixties and purported to raise their children to be open minded and who attended integrated schools, now live in lily-white communities?

I wonder why the Christian "Right" is opposed to abortion, and at the same time passionately supportive of capital punishment. Doesn't the sixth commandment say "Thou shalt not kill" mean everybody? Tell me why, according to "born-again Christians", if God is in the White House, he would authorize a preemptive strike against Iraq, killing and injuring thousands of innocent citizens of Iraq and American soldiers.

What about bearing false witness? Politicians lie to us every day. Tell me why moral values are so important in who gets elected, but after the election, such moral values as availability of health care, an opportunity to work and provide for your family, insurance coverage, a decent wage for low income families is not on the public agenda.

I wonder why gay marriage is a more important issue than raising the minimum wage to help lift people out of poverty, preserving social security for our children, or providing the money that is needed to educate our youth effectively in a global economy. Tell me why. How is gay marriage a greater threat to the institution of marriage than divorce?

## What A Wonderful World This Could Be

What a wonderful world this could be if Christians and people of whatever religious faith, actually remembered and practiced on Monday morning what they heard in their place of worship on Friday, Saturday or Sunday. Sunday morning sermons are about getting along, loving one another, helping the less fortunate, and living the commandments. By the twenty first century, I expected that citizens would have learned to live together in harmony. Have past wars taught us nothing? Why can't we respect and revere our individual differences? Instead we still have racial issues and fears that continue to divide us.

By the twenty first century, I thought our schools would be rich in cultural experiences because our neighborhoods were open and diverse. We still teach the constitution in our schools. It's supposed to be government by the people and for the people. Does that mean some of the people or all of the people? What a wonderful world this could be if we remembered our connectedness and how important it is to take care of those who have the least. Not to let money rule how you think, live, love and feel.

# Cynthia

## Different Strokes for Different Folks

I grew up in an environment where children were not to get in grown folks business. That meant you didn't ask personal questions, like how much you paid for that, how much do you make, what do you do? Imagine, if you can, the hurdle I then had to overcome, as a rookie sales rep, when I had to ask "grown folks" (customers) questions like the size of their budgets? Asking those questions, a requirement in selling, was extremely difficult for me.

My approach was more teaching, by demonstrating the benefits of my product. My philosophy was if you don't have sense enough to buy it, to hell with you. "It's your loss." Of course that doesn't fly. Yet, I've been in sales for more than eighteen years now. How did I get here? This was clearly not the direction I had aimed myself in. Even as a child, my daddy sold my flower seeds and my Girl Scout cookies for me. He even sold my calendars when I was a Brownie. I can negotiate, but I just can't sell. I don't really want to.

My brother, on the other hand, started selling anything he could get his hands on in kindergarten. He started with flower and vegetable seeds and eventually sold homemade perfume and shares of stock for his junior achievement company. He's still selling today. It's in his blood.

I don't even like sales people. You know the kind of sales people who can sell ice to an Eskimo. Shysters! We all know Eskimos don't need ice. What they need is Dr. Scholl's foot warmers! And don't even think about calling me in the evening with that pretend "I care about you" voice asking me how I'm doing tonight! I just might tell you. And it's not likely to be that polite "fine" you're looking for. And still, I've been in sales myself for eighteen years.

## Another Love TKO

National PrePaid was a telephone business my husband and I once owned. Those were the bad years. We tried to provide phone service to customers who have had financial problems with traditional phone companies. We considered this a sound business proposition, as there were many under-served populations in the community who needed a good phone provider. Problem was, they didn't pay us either. Mistake number one, both of us are "softies". We didn't cut 'em off like Ma Bell would have. Alas, no good deed goes unpunished.

We should have been stronger like the big boys. After all we had to pay the big boys for the service whether our broke-ass customers paid us or not. Mistake number two, not pulling the plug sooner. We have used up most of our savings to keep the business afloat. Now both of us are heading toward fifty-five with nothing to show for it. Well, maybe nothing is a slight exaggeration. We do have some proud achievements. Both of our sons attended college even after losing their partial athletic scholarships. One graduated last year and is happily employed. Our second son will graduate in a year. We've managed to refinance the house at a lower interest rate, which replenished some much-needed capital.

I'm freelancing now, making less than a third of what had been the income I was accustomed to grossing in corporate America. My husband is working as a consultant, translation: "no health benefits", and for a fraction of what used to be his income. And it's anybody's guess what bills get paid in any given month. Even with all that, I am less stressed than I have been in a long, long time. I have two wonderful clients who pay my invoices and two wonderful clients who don't! I plan to fire them! I'm no longer a softy. I'm waiting to hear on a couple of proposals and maybe a full-time job. If they come to fruition, I'll have half a dozen clients. That's enough for me now. My husband and I have more time for each other and we're enjoying it. There aren't many couples who can honestly say that all their problems will go away with money. I guess that means we're blessed.

# Sandra

## Big Girls Don't Cry

I had surgery the summer after my high school graduation. This was very painful to me as it resulted in my having to start college in January. Ultimately, I lost my scholarships and had to watch as all my friends left for school in the fall of 1963. My college of attendance was not my first choice, but was selected because I would be only one and a half hours from my surgeon. I'm a big girl, so I took the hand that life dealt me and moved on.

My first ace was trumped, but at least I still had a life thanks to the surgery. While attending Northern Illinois University, my career choice was to be a doctor. I took all the prerequisites such as physiology and chemistry, living the dream until the realization that my parents could not afford to send me to medical school slapped me back into reality. So I gave up this dream, not recognizing that typical medical students went to school on loans. This is where a "real" counselor could have been a help instead of the administrative types that just give you ten minutes to select next semester's courses.

Their vision was never more futuristic than five or six months. Mine was five or six years. My counselor didn't much care what I wanted to do in life or even if I graduated. He was going through the motions, slow motion. His sole purpose in life was to get me enrolled in courses for next semester. It was time to deal myself another hand.

## Don't Kill That Roach

Bugs never bugged me. I've always loved insects and creepy crawly things. My next potential career took a while to name, as I didn't know for sure what kind of job allowed you to work with bugs. I discovered it was entomology, a branch of zoology that deals with insects. I was so excited until I learned that careers in entomology mostly focused on killing my beloved bugs! So I decided to develop a hobby in the study of insects instead.

My favorite bugs are beetles and butterflies. They have the best faces with human-like expressions. I bet you never noticed! My favorite all time movie is "The Fly" with Vincent Price. This interest, however, would not pay the bills, so it was time for another reality check.

## Don't Know Much about History

So, I became a middle school Biology teacher, a career that I found most satisfying for several years. My husband and I married before he finished college. So, when he decided to return to school, I did also, this time planning an advanced degree in Wildlife Biology. I thought I might be a public relations spokesperson for the Audubon Society; bring wildlife to the city, those detached from the "out of doors" world.

Then another dose of reality struck. My marriage of seven years ended and there I was single with two children. Now I had to give up the graduate student stipend, get a full time job and make some rather earth shattering decisions. Thus, ended another dream and a start of something new for me. I became one adult taking care of two children and herself. I won't refer to myself as a single mother as that phrase is entirely too limiting.

## If We Could Start Anew

Unexpectedly, I relocated to Illinois and moved in with a girlfriend, her husband and their child. Over night, their family doubled in size. It took three years and a series of dead-end jobs: day-to-day substitute teaching; a cadre sub; a full time basis substitute; a production supervisor at a factory; and an interview as a cocktail waitress; before I finally found my new life. I'm thankful I didn't get the waitress job!

The move to Illinois, eventually, opened new doors to me; one door being that to corporate America. I finally landed at a large pharmaceutical company as a sales representative where I spent the next twenty-one years of my professional life. This job was a good fit for me as it was related to medicine, my first love. I got to talk with doctors on a daily basis. It provided flexibility, paid the bills and I didn't have to kill any bugs. All those who helped me during this transition are still central in my life today, twenty-five plus years later.

## The Thrill is Gone

The first four years in pharmaceutical were great. I was quite successful winning sales awards and trips, making the "all star" team several times. This enabled me to take my mother on trips to Hawaii and Europe. She would never have otherwise had the opportunity to do. Despite the All Star Team selections, I was never given an outstanding performance rating from my managers, any of them. This was difficult to come to terms with and still haunts me on days when I allow my mind to wander into that neverland.

In time, when I was promoted to manager, I was exposed to the real corporate culture of this company. Now that I was "inside", I began to notice the traditional, conservative, white, male environmental behavior of my company. As a manager, I was exposed to and became much more aware of the inequities. For example, traditionally the first line managers spoke at the national kick off meetings. This, I greatly looked forward to as an opportunity to speak to reps in the field and become a role model for them.

I would have been the first role model woman of color. It was not to happen. Mysteriously, my presentation was cut from the agenda. It went down hill from there for me. The person responsible for this action was ironically the same person whose position I filled when I first joined the company. It would be later that I discovered a number of unethical behaviors about her. For one, she shared her home with a key user of one of our top promoted products. Use your imagination on how that story goes.

As I assumed her territory, my first year out, she left a large return that I had to "eat". That left me with a bad taste so to speak. And in the end, she became the last manager that I worked for. Neither of us could get past our unspoken history together. When my father died, she merely sent a plant. Though she lived a few minutes away, she never phoned or visited with me during that time. She's still employed by the company. Eventually, I was downsized, but I can breathe again as you will see in my story below.

## Smiling Faces Sometimes They Don't Tell the Truth

I continued for years having excellent sales successes for which I was not rewarded. Smiling faces everywhere you look can give you a false sense of security. I thought my job was secure since my sales were soaring. My next position was back in the field promoting a new product. It was touted as a prestigious position, yet the offer was bottom line, less money. Did I have "fool" stamped on my forehead? By now, I was becoming more outspoken in my dissatisfaction of the status quo. I was, after all, retirement eligible. Retirement eligible status certainly does a lot for one's courage. It loosed my lips, which were never that tight to begin with.

I tried to champion the Black Cardiologist Association and HIV Aids programs for donations from my company hoping to have an impact in the minority community. When it became clear to me that they were never going to recognize the need, nor support causes in these communities, I stewed over it for about ten months. Then, I decided to jump ship. Fortunately, I was working in the era of downsizing, right sizing, redeployment and reorganization. When they offered me the package, I kissed the corporate world good bye.

Now I'm paid to "rant and rave" and I'm loving it. I became grounded in faith and pro-choice as soon as I knew what both meant. As the State coordinator for the religious coalition for reproductive choice, I am truly paid to rant. I get to say what I think without fear of retribution. What a job! Thank you for letting me be myself.

# Susan

## Ain't No Mountain High Enough

My first career was never what I would call a satisfying one. It paid the bills and covered a vacation a year. Except, it just didn't offer the feeling of accomplishment or success I desired. I think many black people are underemployed or undervalued in their places of employment. It's one reason why black organizations like The Links, sororities and fraternities continue to play an important role in our communities.

They not only provide scholarships, support and help to those who have been less financially successful, but they are a significant opportunity for the much-needed gratification and recognition that black folks are missing in the work place. They provide an opportunity for leadership, accomplishment and respect for one's knowledge and expertise.

That's the part of you the boss never seems to recognize. Ever had your boss compliment you on an effort by saying something like, "Good job", Glad to have you on the team", "You really stepped up to the plate, etc."? When they do, it's almost like it was an accident, not anticipated, and he or she was pleasantly surprised with your contribution. They don't know JACK! I'm all that and a cup of coffee.

My newest career is in real estate sales. The office is made up mostly of rich bored wives who need something to do while their husbands are traveling or working long hours. Year after year, I have watched them receive recognition for sales accomplishments topping two hundred and fifty or five hundred thousand dollars, while I hover between one and two hundred thousand in commissions. Of course, the difference is they sell two or three homes of friends or acquaintances valued at millions while I'm out hustling much smaller homes for sale in my market.

This year I topped the two hundred and fifty thousand dollar mark to the jaw dropping expressions of the entire office. And I did it one small to medium sized house at a time. I feel exonerated and exhilarated at the same time. "Oh yes it's ladies night and the feelings right."

# Carla

## You Can't Hide From Yourself. Everywhere You Go. There You Are.

Let me begin by saying, "Don't let other people's racism ruin your life." Sometimes we as a people internalize hatred of self. We start to identify with the oppressor. In reality, it's their problem not ours. It's not about you. In the 1970s, a large computer company that I worked for was experimenting with hiring people of color in larger numbers. So after they hired me, they hired Steve. They assumed Steve would do well since his dad was a successful businessman in the community. Steve was put through the same branch office pre-training program that I had and was sent off to school.

This was to be seven weeks of intense training in Texas. Upon arrival, all new trainees had to pass the entrance exam, or return to their respective branch offices. Steve failed. Management didn't quite know what to do with this result, so they told Steve to work harder and sent him back in two weeks. He passed on this second try, however, didn't do especially well in the seven week class itself.

Upon return to the branch office, Steve was assigned to an experienced sales representative of mediocre success in our office. During the next two years of training, rookie sales reps were to be mentored ostensibly to gain the experience needed to become independent and successful account managers. Steve's, so-called assigned mentor, basically gave him administrative tasks to do, like financial analysis on customer accounts.

For six months, Steve sat in the office doing meaningless paperwork. He was never invited to attend customer calls with his mentor, where the real action takes place. He was not getting the development needed to become a good sales person. He was not doing presentations, calling on customers or providing product demonstrations. These are all skills a successful sales rep should have. I observed this situation from afar and considered carefully what my reaction would be.

Sometimes we are guilty of reducing Dr. Martin Luther King Jr.'s message to a simple "dream" when we can do more than dream. His life was about much more than a dream. We can accomplish. So even though technically, this was none of my business, I decided to talk with my manager about Steve's situation. In two years, management would have to assign Steve to a solo territory where he would be on his own without the background experience he desperately needed for success.

I suggested to my manager that Steve be assigned to a better salesman with the opportunity to truly learn how to manage a territory. If this did not occur, Steve would either fail or be fired. Either way the manager would have to explain why. Especially since the company had a two year investment in Steve. I didn't say to him, "You're letting your racism and trepidation keep you from supporting Steve in a more positive way," though it was surely tempting.

Two weeks later my manager had me share my thoughts with the branch manager. Two weeks after that, Steve was reassigned to a better salesman and a better experience. The end of this story is not quite the end. Steve did become a "star". His reward was to be assigned the dormant accounts as his first independent sales territory. Dormant accounts are customers who have stopped buying from the company or have never bought from the company.

Steve, being the star that he was, brought in new orders from these previously dead accounts. Big orders! Had he continued to be ignored, he probably would have been fired. As it turned out, he was a big asset to the branch. Two years later, Steve left the company to work for his father. A good move for him and a real loss to the company as admitted by his manager who told Steve, "If you ever want to come back…" Now isn't that special. Life isn't always fair. When you learn that lesson you've finally grown up.

# Maryann

## Kind of a Drag

I never wanted to work a real job. I started college to find a husband, period. My expectation was that he would be a doctor, lawyer, or some highly paid professional who would be able to take care of me and our children. I met him, the love of my life, at a party Labor Day weekend. We were so in love that by December I was carrying his Christmas present and it wasn't under the tree.

So we married on New Years Day, 1967 and on July 15th our first son was born. We were young and apparently not very good in the use of birth control so by the next May our second son was born. With us now supporting two children and neither of us with a degree, everybody had to make a financial contribution to the household for the sake of survival. I had to find work. That was when I decided to sell Amway products.

The sales leader said I could make a ton of money with very little effort. That's exactly what I put into the job, very little effort. I tried calling my friends, except what did they need with cleaning products? They lived in dorm rooms. I nearly drove the old folks at church crazy on Sundays, who didn't understand the pyramid marketing strategy. They were supposed to fill their closets with product to sell so I could make money just sitting down!

Instead, we were still broke and I had a closet full of Amway products. Next, I tried being a part-time sales associate at a downtown Chicago retail store. This would be great with the clothing discounts possible. The boys and I were fashion show ready everyday. Problem was, by the time I paid for the sitter, transportation to work, lunch and the credit card bill that I managed to max out every month, there was precious little money left for our other bills.

What happened to paradise? My life was not going according to plan. In the beginning it was fun, after a while it was a drag and in the end we had to move back home with my parents. I went back to school. I needed a real job.

Today I'm a mortgage banker. The best part about it is bankers' hours, of course, and my clients come to me. I don't have to beat the bushes trying to sell something nobody wants or needs. I do feel a sense of accomplishment when I can help young families achieve their dream of home ownership. In fact, I work extra hard with young, broke, just starting out couples. I know their lives. It used to be mine.

# Chapter Four

# Everybody Loves Somebody

*I've Been Married Most Of My Life*

# Arlene

## The Hunter Gets Captured by the Game

I expected to work a while and then become a woman of leisure, a fifties kind of mother like Donna Reed or June Cleaver. This was the standard by which we were raised through the media. I first met my husband at a Northwestern University campus party one weekend while home from college. This was a brief encounter, minimally capturing each other's attention. It would be one year later, before he actually called me for a date.

As a senior, I was home from college for nine weeks to complete student teaching. He called me late one evening and declared, "You must not be busy since you're home at eight o'clock on a Saturday night…". I, of course was insulted at the insinuation, so I refused his invitation for a date that evening. I was tired and didn't feel like getting to know someone new anyway.

The vague memory of his handsome face did encourage me to invite him over the next evening, as sort of a consolation. As luck would have it, I had a previous engagement on Sunday, from which I was late returning. Poor guy had to sit and make small talk with my parents for about an hour before I returned home. He was friendly, and at the same time, not amused upon my late entry into the living room. Being the big basketball star that he was at Northwestern, he was not accustomed to this kind of treatment, one of indifference on the part of a woman, especially one he hardly knew.

He was used to getting what he wanted, when he wanted, for the most part. At this time in my life, I had become disenchanted with basketball players and athletes in general. These old school "players" were too much play for me. I didn't particularly trust this new basketball player that would eventually become part of my life.

My father was the one who actually encouraged me to give him a chance.

What I didn't know at the time, and for some years later, was that my father was working behind the scenes. He was worried that since I hadn't brought home anyone special or even talked of anyone special at school, I might never marry. It was common practice in the sixties to get an education and a husband while attending college. There were weekly serenades in the dorm celebrating other girls becoming pinned or engaged. I was getting the education and my parents were proud of that. However, there was no man, no future husband in my life at least that they could see.

My father never said a word to me about his concern. I was a college senior majoring in Elementary Education. In that environment, the hopes of even meeting a man in the future seemed dim, at least at work. I guess my parents thought the only place I would meet a future husband would be at school or through work. They hadn't known me to go clubbing or such. In most cases, the only men in an elementary school building were the janitor and the principal. The principal was always married, with children, as he was generally an experienced person and therefore older. And of course, they didn't pay for my education, to end up marrying the janitor.

Being the protective parent that he was, my father mentioned to a friend of his who worked at Northwestern University, who mentioned to my *future* husband, that a girlfriend and I were home student teaching. Consequently, the phone call late on that Saturday night occurred. Annoyed by my attitude, my *future* husband decided he would initiate the chase with a plan of dropping the "game" once captured. Well six months later we were engaged. And thirty-seven years later we are still happily married. The hunter was captured by the game. To this day he still believes he had to convince ME to marry him. Men, what do they really know? I chose him!

In fact, I must admit that "Nothin' Like I Thought" does not apply to my marriage. The one thing in my life that is everything that I hoped for and looked for in a man, I found in my husband. He has been a stable force and good provider. Without him, weathering the various storms of life would have been a lot more life threatening. He has lived up to my expectations. I got just want I wanted.

## Super Woman

It's been three different marriages over the more than thirty years and not surprisingly....I am no June Cleaver. Goals change, people change, what you need changes. As I said earlier, in my fantasy, I expected to live June Cleaver's life, complete with pearls as I vacuumed the living room. Well that didn't happen. Womanhood for black women is different from white women to begin with. We have always been part of the workforce since slavery. It was required in slavery and then mandated through Jim Crow laws. There was never the work versus stay-at-home mom conflict among black women. Work was pretty much a necessity.

When my husband and I married, my dream was to work until I gave birth and then I would stay at home and raise the children. We found out early in the marriage, like two months in, that wouldn't happen either. My husband went to work and I was home alone for a mere three weeks before my new job as a teacher started. I nearly drove us both crazy.

There was no way I would become June Cleaver at home cleaning, baking, and awaiting my darling husband's arrival from a hard day at the office. I could clean our four-room apartment twice and still only use up an hour in the day. Clearly, I needed adult interaction. And I needed it fairly regularly. And my husband needed more than someone looking lovely when he returned home for dinner.

Like most black women, I had to be there with a sympathetic and understanding ear for my husband when he came home from work, with the "how the MAN had mistreated a brother again today" story. It was not easy breaking the color barrier of the sixties in corporate America. My sistas know what I am talking about and so do you after reading the previous chapter.

Additionally, I discovered that what I needed was to be productive and feel like I was making a contribution to society. So, even when our children were young, I continued to work part-time, two to three days a week. I tried my best to be all things to all people, a good wife and mother, teacher, student, daughter, friend and like so many before, a community volunteer working for the cause.

## You're All I Need

After one year of marriage, my husband was drafted into the army. We were vacationing on the East coast when word came from my sister. There was a letter from Uncle Sam addressed to my husband. In the sixties we had a draft lottery system and his number, one of the last to be drawn during the Vietnam War era, was up. Despite his flat feet and height of six feet, six inches, he was bound for the rice patties.

This would be a target no Viet Cong could miss in daylight, so he enlisted in the Navy flight program instead, following a childhood dream to become a pilot. Becoming the pilot was easy. It was like a perpetual vacation. He would fly in the morning, study at night and we would spend afternoons at the beach. Friday night was bid whist, a well-known card game night. Saturday nights were spent at the movies, with the same friends from Friday night.

It was a piece of cake, so long as we could avoid the base security that always seemed to find fault with a black man driving a corvette with a fair skinned woman. To them, I guess, I looked a little too light, maybe "white" from a distance. So, becoming an "officer and a gentleman" was a little harder in Florida during the sixties.

On one occasion, prior to his commissioning, I traveled to Pensacola, Florida to attend the Officers Candidates' Ball with my husband. All Navy bases have golf courses on them so we entered the security gate, and slowly drove the four or five mile entrance to the base enjoying the view of the greens and grounds. We noticed there seemed to be someone following us as we wound our way through, paying little attention.

At some point, he pulled us over announcing himself as the base security. That meant he was real important and to be respected! He looked in the car, my husband dressed in his formal whites, complete with sword, and me in my evening gown, and stated with white man authority, "You git smart with me and I'll give you a ticket." Then he went back to his car and sat down.

We waited for what seemed to be fifteen or twenty minutes with no action on his part. Finally, my husband, not knowing what else to do, got out of the car and asked if he was going to issue a ticket or what. "I told you if you got smart with me I'd give you a ticket," he yelled and commenced to writing. This would be the first of three unnecessary encounters with the base security.

Becoming the wife of "an officer and a gentleman" should also have been easy, but it turned out to be difficult and not nearly as much fun as I had hoped. While my husband was in boot camp, the Navy sent me a book on how to be an officer's wife. I thought I knew as much; however, the book said otherwise. To think they have a code of behavior all written down for the wife of an officer. It described what I was to wear and when and with whom I was and was not to fraternize.

The Navy's flight program had token-black candidates, which was challenging when it came to socializing, as officers were not to be too friendly with enlisted men. So, if the fellow white officers are not exactly asking to be your best friend, and the black guys, save a couple of other pilots, are marines and mostly enlisted, what would be the most logical option? There was never more than one African American per officers' candidate school class. We walked a fine line and commenced to fraternize with the enlisted couples.

The teas I attended with the other gloved and coiffed officers' wives I found to be cold and unfriendly. The only warm thing in the room was the cup of tea. With few exceptions, I felt completely alone in a room filled with smiling, haughty women. This was an odd circumstance, for me, as I had attended integrated schools and joined an integrated sorority in college, so I expected better. I had always had white friends so I anticipated it would be no different in Pensacola, Florida. Tea parties were very different south of the Mason Dixie line.

At my husband's commissioning ceremony, I wore a bright orange knit dress with orange suede boots and a big, fluffy, auburn Afro wig. I was not trying to make a statement; I was just being me. I guess we both knew then, I was not destined to be an officer's wife. With the war winding down in the early seventies, we gratefully received an early out and headed back to Chi-town.

## When I Became of Age…

The early years of marriage are youthful, energetic, career-oriented times, full of exploration and learning. We learn about each other, life, wants and desires. While we are making lots of friends, having fun partying, time flies.

At twenty-four I joined a women's baseball team. Just a bunch of us out to have fun thinking baseball would be a good form of exercise. We called ourselves the Park Forest South Fillies. At some point it did become important to win, maybe after losing really badly, our first three games. So we decided we needed a coach, a free one.

My husband was drafted for the job. After observing us practice, he gave us the following advice. "Do the best you can when fielding the ball to stay ahead of the runner or throw the ball to the pitcher." That usually will end the play in polite women's baseball. Then, he said, "You babes aren't all that good, except, neither is the competition. So here is what you do…if you manage to hit the ball, just keep running."

The logic of this suggestion became apparent, as we discovered that in continuing to run after hitting a single, the other team would become confused, not knowing where to throw the ball. They had not had the benefit of my husband's first piece of advice. Most of the time the opposing teams would throw behind the runner, causing errors, which ultimately resulted in our team scoring multiple runs. Bottom line was, they never knew where to throw the ball.

So singles became doubles, doubles became home runs and so on. We would often win by twenty or more runs. You can get a lot of exercise running bases! Our dugout was wild with excitement and crazy made up cheers. Anyone observing this display would be hard pressed to believe this was a group of adult professional women. The other teams hated us. And a good time was had by all, by all of us anyway.

We thought we would have forever and before we knew it we were turning thirty. I married rather young at twenty two, which means I never lived alone or on my own before marriage, unless you count the time in college. This is not necessarily a bad thing, if you grow to learn that you can make it on your own, if necessary. Every woman needs to know that for herself. Many women from earlier generations and mine did not learn this lesson and were afraid to leave bad marriages. It's not that you want that story to be yours but as a good Girl Scout, one must always be prepared.

## Easier Said Than Done

As I approached thirty, I started to sense that life was passing me by. I hadn't, in my assessment, made a difference, made a name for myself, successfully represented the family or just plain done a lot of things I thought I would have done by this time in my life. Approaching ten years after graduation and what had happened to all those dreams of being "somebody"? I imagined, in one of my past lives, that I had been a star of stage and screen.

This explained my love of dancing and singing the lyrics to all my favorite songs on the radio; thus, the birth of the world's oldest teenager, as my husband continues to refer to me today. I signed up for tap lessons, jazzercise, horseback riding lessons and graduate school. I started jogging and competing in ten K races on weekends. This satisfied me for a while. Then I took a larger step.

It began with the running of a friend's campaign as he sought a local office in our village. I organized his meetings, conferences, coffees, and campaign speeches. This was fun, and akin to my high school years, was a role in the wings, not center stage. Real satisfaction would elude me until I, myself, ran as part of the Democratic ticket for Monee Township trustee.

Monee Township was no Chicago, but it was big enough for me. I found an avenue that provided me with an opportunity to not only feel like I was somebody as Jesse Jackson rehearsed us to say, but to also serve. We served a small community, and we served it honestly and well. People in need had needs met. The food pantry when depleted was restocked, ready before the need arose again. It wasn't about us or money or the politically connected. It was about community and service.

## A House is Not a Home

The next phase of marriage brings more focus, or at least the focus changes. The children come, whether by birth or adoption. A house is not automatically a home. You have to make it one. Life becomes about the children, their needs, wants, desires and school. In phase two of our marriage, my husband and I took on new identities and other people's kids too. He was the coach and I was team mother. He had scout duty while I became room mother, van pool driver, chauffeur, tutor, referee, teacher, maid, cook, nurse, Jack & Jill mom and whatever it took to raise our kids "right".

It gets confusing. Some days you aren't quite sure who you are supposed to be. Maybe that's why when asked at school what his parents did for a living, our son replied, "daddy works with computers and mommy watches cartoons!" I can't begin to say where that idea came from. The kids seem to multiply on you as well. We had two, but it seemed like four. Some days I set the table for six. There was myself, my husband, our daughter Pamela, our son Jeffrey and two other people named *I forgot* and *I don't know*. That's how those two people answered almost every question posed by the parents. Question: "Where's your homework?" Answer: "I forgot." Question: "Who left the water running." Answer: "I don't know." It was never ending.

I tried to jog every day just to have some alone time. In the middle of all those identities you are still a wife every day. Somehow husbands need more during this time and you seem to have less for them. The kids sap all the energy you have. I was lucky. My husband helped with chores. His manhood wasn't challenged by domesticity. He was brave enough to pick up the vacuum cleaner, cook, stay home with a sick child and help with homework. Where was the Internet when we really needed it? Homework was the same old boring assignments we did in school. Except for a few new faces, no more Dick and Jane, the workbook activities look identical.

I've learned that no matter how long you're married, it still takes a partnership and commitment. It's critical not to forget about each other during the raising of the children phase. With all the energy raising the kids requires you don't want your husband going elsewhere for time and attention. After all he was your first-born!

Husbands receive a lot of special attention initially in a marriage. I tried new recipes every week and spent a great deal of time making the house look clean and special for him. I had a distinctive sauce or gravy for every dish. Even though this behavior waned after a time, we used to make sure we spent time together continuing to "date" even after several years in the marriage.

A date might include dessert and the theatre or just a movie and popcorn. On no particular occasion, maybe a Wednesday night, I would use the "good" dishes, (i.e. the china and stemware) for dinner. Along with candles, this would make for a special dinner table even if the menu was soup and grilled cheese sandwiches.

## This Time is My Time This Time is Your Time ...

As I've said, by the mid thirties, my life was not my own. It belonged to my kids, their schedule of school, games, social life, homework, lessons and insatiable need for money. This mainly happened because we were later than many of our friends in starting a family. Isn't it funny how your children's assignments and projects are the same ones you did in school? Remember those leaf projects, shadow boxes, storyboards, English term papers? We should have saved that stuff and recycled!

Truthfully, our children needed tutoring in most subjects and as the "teacher" in the household, I was expected to provide it. That was a mistake. I was angry and disappointed when they didn't "get it" and they recognized that even when I tried my best to mask those feelings. A mother should never be in that position with her children, which could result in their self-esteem being damaged. We're supposed to make everything "all better".

Alas, those were the days when Sylvan and private tutoring were beyond our budget, so my husband and I have spent hours and hours working with our kids on book reports and other assignments. We thought we were demonstrating the value in learning for learning's sake, not just to get a good grade. Turns out our children were interested in neither. When does the change happen? Children start kindergarten so eager and excited to learn and then at some point many seem to lose interest, lose motivation and ultimately lose the excitement. This is a topic, which deserves further exploration with JACK.

## When a Man Loves a Woman

Marriage can be a good trip, they say, if you take along the proper luggage. Fortunately for me, I had the right luggage. My husband comes home after work, does laundry if needed and respects my community involvement even though it takes time away from "us". The marriage hasn't been perfect, though to others looking in from the outside, it may have looked that way. He has always been considerate, respectful and committed to the marriage. He's perfect most of the time. You know even a saint can get on your nerves once in a while.

I know I've rocked his boat now and again too. We've exchanged angry words, threatened to leave, but always decided to work through whatever the issue was, correct the error, forgive or just let it go. At times we probably could have used counseling, but like most folks' husbands, he didn't want an outsider in "his business". We've made adjustments to and for each other as time has passed because we were both dedicated to the marriage.

## Stop in the Name of Love

We agreed early in the marriage to never go to bed angry at each other. Well, after thirty-seven years, it's safe to say that didn't always happen. And at the same time, we.didn't let anger linger for long. We try to deal only with the current situation, when we have disagreements. There have been times (and the older I get, the more there are) when I'm angry with my husband over something that I can't even remember the next day.

I have tried and tried to remember old stuff. "I know I've been upset with you over this very thing before!" "I know I have." "You have done this before!" And he says, "When?" And damn if I can't remember the date, time or circumstances. Drives me nuts! He remembers everything! Makes you want to take notes so you can reference them the next time. But then, where would you keep all those notes? Let the past stay just where it is, in the past. If you can't get past *the past*, then you haven't much future.

Marriage is a serious commitment. It takes working together, compromise and patience. If one puts up with too many things you really don't like early in the marriage, they will haunt you later. Little things can become BIG things as time passes. At times, we found ourselves arguing about stupid things, like cilantro in the salad or reheated chicken "...when you know I hate reheated chicken."

I've learned no matter how important it is to prepare healthy meals, don't ever run out of cookies and Kool-aid in my household. My husband will give up pork chops and ham, if he's supplied with his cookies on a regular basis. Now that's a small thing. Small things are what keep a marriage in tact; like saying I love you just for the heck of it and good night before you go to bed. My husband, to this day, wakes me with a "Good morning gorgeous!" It's nice to wake up next to someone who sees you the way you think you look, despite the years.

## It's a Game of Give and Take

My husband and I are in the third phase now, and are working to make sure we don't end up like some couples who divorce after forty years of marriage. It helps to have some common interests and something to talk about. After a daily healthy dose of Lou Dobbs, Chris Mathews and Keith Olbermann, we are never at a loss for political conversation. Some of our friends aren't nearly as well-versed or interested in current events as we are. They appear to stop talking or at least listening to each other.

I've seen it happen to very close friends. My girlfriend came home from the beauty salon to find a note from her husband saying he was leaving her. In fact he was already gone and without explanation. Since people are living longer these days, they figure there's life after sixty years and maybe it might be better or happier with someone else.

Suddenly single at sixty, now that's scary! My girlfriend had to learn things she took for granted during her forty years of marriage, like how to use a hammer; there's more than one kind of screw driver; file taxes; plan a budget; program the VCR; send e-mail; check the battery; discover where all her assets are located and their value; stuff she just never used to worry about.

## Don't it Make Your Brown Eyes Blue

During this third phase, I have also learned to move into a different phase of life that doesn't revolve around who and what my kids are.

Even though report cards were rarely something to celebrate in our household, I had hoped my kids would attend and finish college. They didn't finish and I had to learn to manage that disappointment, and not wrap my ego; my sense of success in their success; or, lack there of. It is, after all, their life now; a result of their choices, whether I agreed with them or not. I'm still working on how to not take on their problems as mine to solve…a work in progress.

My daughter and I have bi-weekly financial sessions, where I oversee the paying of her bills and the balancing of her checkbook. This, of course, is to prevent future errors based on prior experiences. Despite my efforts, the errors still occur and I am beginning to think they are not accidental. I've recently discovered that my son needs the same lessons and he is four years older than she. Even with this supervision, she still manages to overwrite the checkbook regularly.

This is mostly due to the use of a debit card for which deductions are never recorded in a timely fashion, if ever. It's like free money to her, though I think she knows better. She still loans money she doesn't have to friends in need. Isn't that kind and generous of her? Guess who has to make up the difference when she's short on her own bills as a result? Insurance will go unpaid as one hundred dollars is spent on a hairweave and nails.

I know I am not alone in this story! I've had to figure out how to have a positive relationship with my children, no matter what path they have taken. This has sometimes been difficult, as my husband and I have varying views on adult children and how your relationship should be with them. They swing from spoiling them with unconditional support, to "divorcing" them and letting them go. On any given day, either of us may hold either view.

We still provide support to each other by pulling the other in "off the ledge" on those occasions where one kid has managed to drive us to a point of what seems to be no return. If only there was a magic pill for this.

There are so many examples of "ledge" incidents that it's hard to choose just one. Recently, Pam announced that her job position might be downsized at her place of work. Our response was to put the full court press on finding another job before the current one ends. That meant posting resumes on Monster.com and following up on leads. This effort began with a painstaking two-hour effort to update her resume and a discussion on the importance of physical appearance during interviews.

Our daughter has a tendency for what we consider the extreme in appearance and I thought I had gained concurrence with her, the idea of displaying temporarily a more mainstream look, until at least the new job had been secured. The next day after this discussion, she stopped by our home to pick up extra resumes for distribution. She was sporting a new hairstyle of long, flowing, wavy blond weave, crowned two inches from roots that were partially strawberry blond (orange) and her own natural hair, which is black.

What part of looking mainstream did she not understand from our discussion the previous evening? My husband sent me the *count to ten before screaming and choking* look, which was partially helpful. On most occasions, the best approach has been for the one who is about to "blow" to leave the room and let the other pick up the conversation from that point forward.

Pam is a communicator, calling sometimes three or four times a day. Jeffrey, on the other hand, avoids communication if at all possible, a passive aggressive form of behavior. He lives out of state, is underemployed and therefore still somewhat financially dependent on the parents. The lack of communication is one way he avoids parental check ups, which at the age of thirty-one, no one would want to endure. So his father leaves a dozen messages before he returns the calls, usually with some lame excuse as to why he couldn't get back to him right away.

The really annoying factor associated with this behavior is the reality that he would not even have a phone if it weren't in his father's name to begin with, a status which will remain until his past phone bills are paid and his credit rating is improved. The dilemma of divergent expectations, in this deal, sends us both to the ledge, holding on to each other to keep from jumping. So we pray. It's easy to pray and harder to believe the prayer was heard, and harder still to believe it will be answered. So we pray again.

# Susan

## He's so Fine

You know how they say you better watch out for the milkman?
Well, I married the milkman's son. My daddy advised me not to do
it. But since I had something cookin' in the oven, I thought it best to
go ahead and marry him. Six months later our son was born. Six
pounds, nine ounces looking up at me for answers I know I don't
have. He was a really great kid. Though he physically looks like my
husband, he is nothing like his father.

When we married, I had high hopes even though it wasn't exactly
planned. It turns out that I didn't just marry the milkman's son, I
married his mother too. Having no money, we were forced to live with
the in-laws for nine months. My mother-in-law was a very pretty
woman and accustomed to being the center of attention. My moving
in presented competition. No decisions were made without her input
and approval. I was young, but old enough to realize more than one
mother in a household spells trouble. When the baby came out, we got
out and I mistakenly thought that would end the madness.

We moved into a home of our own, except it felt like a hotel. Every
weekend the in-laws came over and spent the entire weekend with
us. What were they thinking? Even though I finally had my own
home, I was still not the "woman" of the home. My mother-in-law
showed up the first day after the move and reorganized my kitchen
cabinets. Whenever I complained to my husband about her interference, to my shock and surprise, he took her side! I should have
recognized immediately that this marriage was doomed.

She was a sweet, cunning and masterful manipulator. My husband
was her "favorite" and she was the number one woman in his life. I
had no say and little control. His parents even accompanied us on

vacations. Once I planned a three-week camping trip, thinking for sure she would stay home avoiding the heat and insects. Before I knew it, she had purchased a ticket! They traveled on many trips with us throughout the years, the basis of many battles between the favored son and me. He continues to cater to her to this day. Being "married" to both of us, I think contributed ultimately to his drinking problem.

One unplanned event can lead to a series of unplanned events until things get totally out of control. It took a while, but I finally figured out the plan for my life and started to work my plan. That plan did not include his mother. And eventually it didn't include my husband either. After a long sixteen years, I put all of them out of my house. When the kids finished high school, I left the state. Just so you know, cream doesn't always rise to the top. My "X" looked like cream, tasted like cream, but I'll be dog gone if he didn't just sour like old milk. I divorced him sixteen years later and I didn't cry over spilt milk.

# Sandra

## Bye Bye Love

I married the first time at twenty to my high school sweetheart. He would be the father of my children. I thought our marriage would last a lifetime. He was so caring and attentive. He noticed everything about me. At the time I thought that was a good thing. He used to choose my clothes, offer opinions about various things like my hairstyles and the glasses I wore. I thought, he must really love me to be so assiduous.

The life I envisioned was akin to Donna Reed, though I never really wanted to be a stay at home wife, a "desperate housewife". I wanted financial security, the grand house, weekends attending art events and parties. The plan was to marry, raise the children, watch the children marry and have grandchildren. The cycle of life would go merrily along. It didn't, he wouldn't, they couldn't, so I did and life is what it is.

## For Your Precious Love

For his precious love, at twenty, I thought I would do anything. At first I felt like a bird on a pedestal. Later it became more like a bird in a cage. He was constantly clipping my wings, denying me opportunity for growth and expression. I had to ask permission to go places and even to participate in professional activities. The attention became oppression. I needed more freedom, so at thirty, I left. Afraid, but not alone, I moved on, to another state, another career, another life.

My girlfriends safely kept me from becoming a wounded bird. They took me in, fed me and my children, encouraged me and helped me find a job. Somewhere in the process I grew up. This bird learned to fly, to soar! At forty, I had reinvented myself three times over. I discovered talents I didn't think I had, like public speaking. And, I've found love again, though not necessarily a husband. Who knew?

Most people assumed that I was through with men when I left my husband and moved to Illinois. Having married young, before I finished college, I had never been a single adult. I had never known other men, so this new found single life represented an opportunity to me. So I partied a bit, as much as a mother of two young children can do. I've had several relationships, but from Arthur to Raymond to Nelson to Robert, I don't think I'll ever find true love; at least the marrying kind again. I want too much (some people say) and I'll never really find it.

I have a list of what I'm looking for in a relationship, a future husband. I tend to evaluate the qualities each man has initially, seeing mostly the positive, until it goes downhill. I stay in the relationship until I just don't want to any more. I probably have an invisible shield up now to avoid any more pain or disappointment. So far no one has measured up to my list of characteristics that the perfect future husband must have. He's probably not really out there. At this point I'm not interested in compromise, nor going hunting either. I enjoy my life just the way it is.

# Mavis

## Neither One of Us Wants to be the First to Say Good-bye

I question why I got married so young. In my day, I guess it was expected. You married for security and to get out of the house. When I was young, women just didn't move out and live on their own. I thought my husband and I had a lot in common, common goals that would bind us together forever. All we knew at the time, we had in common. Reflecting back, we didn't know much. We grew up together and learned together in what I thought was a happy marriage. I was happy.

Two people can grow at different levels and at different times, but if you are committed to each other, then you do not always have to be at the same level at the same time. I would never have considered being with another man sexually other than my husband. I know that I was a bit conservative and not much of a risk taker like many women today. I expected my husband would be there and we would take care of each other forever. Then one day, he just up and left.

## The Jerk

We are now divorced after forty years of marriage and today I wonder what part of marriage was truth and what was a lie. You just don't think after forty years it can happen to you! I thought my husband was honest and fair. Everything we had was built together through hard work. I spoiled him, waiting on him hand and foot. I even combed his hair while he ate breakfast. Yet at the time of our divorce it was his opinion that my contribution to the marriage, financially and otherwise, was remarkably less than his.

He gives new definition to a "senior moment". After all this time, he simply announces that he isn't happy and then he was gone. This, I never noticed from his behavior, since we had continued to celebrate holidays, anniversaries and happy occasions with wonderful gifts and laughs that appeared to be genuine. The last ten years of the marriage, we successfully dealt with a number of his health issues. Was that a result of his unhappiness? Or, was he simply waiting to get healthy enough to divorce me?

If I had known that, I might have done some things differently. There can be clues of trouble in a marriage that you just don't recognize until later. Women need to get better at recognizing the signs. They can be irritations that seem little but represent a whole lot more; small comments you take as jokes; stares that seem to pass right through you. My husband actually said one day, "When I get well, I'm going to divorce you." I thought he was joking. We laughed! HA!

Where is that crystal ball when you need it? If this happens to you, don't lose sleep over the jerk. Just get on with your life. It's too short to dwell on the past. When you're sixty, you have more past than future so just let it go and move forward.

## Someone Should Have Told Me This Wouldn't Last

If given a choice I would still rather grow old with a partner. There are a lot of things I had no intention of learning that I have now had to learn. This has been a stretch for my sixty-year old brain. Did you know you have to remove the clear plastic tape at the bottom of the printer ink cartridge? I didn't until I returned the tape cartridge back to the company twice.

When they sent the replacement cartridge, it didn't print any better. I was so frustrated that I was about to return the printer and the cartridge to the manufacturer as I was reduced to tears! So then I decided to give one last effort by calling the help line. I talked to a service person located in India who spent at least twenty minutes with me to resolve the problem.

He must hear from dummies like me all day long because he was incredibly patient. He stepped me through the type of printer,

printer cartridge and where I purchased everything. He walked me through the installation of the cartridge. I thought I was going the break the damn thing before we finished. Then he asked the most important question that none of his predecessors had thought to even suggest. He asked, "Madam is there a little tab on the bottom of the ink cartridge?" Eureka! "That is the protective tape and if you remove that tape the printer will work just fine." Problem solved. In church that Sunday I said a special blessing for the healing.

Here are a few more things I have had to learn upon becoming *suddenly single at sixty:*

- How to use a computer;
- How to manage money and a budget;
- How to buy a set of tires for my car;
- How to prioritize;
- How to work home electronics like the stereo equipment;
- Survival alone and to be alone with one's self and still be happy and satisfied;
- To identify useful resources;
- To protect oneself during the divorce process;
- Emotional and spiritual strength;
- How to lose anger and help my adult child to lose the anger;
- To be willing to ask for and accept help from others.

I have learned to do things I never liked to do. I never envisioned, for example, washing windows or the car; tightening the screws on the toilet seat. You know that can be important when you plop down with aching knees! Consider the obvious. I can program the VCR, an accomplishment of which I am especially proud. Plenty of girlfriends younger than me can't do that without the assistance of grandchildren. My husband left me and I thought I was lost. In the end I found myself.

# Linda

## Secret Lovers or Who's Zoomin' Who

Funny thing about secrets is, they never are! Someone always knows. Secrets are never safe with anyone, not your best friend, not even your mother. My secret is being told by someone that I had no idea even knew my story for this book. My husband and I have been together since Junior High. We dated exclusively as soon as our parents allowed dating and attended each other's proms. He was my first and I was his. Though we attended separate colleges, neither of us met someone new that we would consider spending the rest of our lives with. So we married one week after graduation.

Twenty-five years, four affairs (his), two affairs and an abortion (mine) later, we are still together. At forty, my husband is still a handsome, soft-spoken man, except, suffering from a major mid-life crisis. His friends are either single, never married or divorced. That alone is problematic. Why couldn't he just buy a sports car? Let me rephrase that, "Why couldn't he just be happy with the sports car he bought?"

## The Freaks Come Out at Night

He started "hanging out" with these friends more frequently as his fortieth birthday approached. The availability of women was more than he could resist. They exercised his ego and apparently had more to offer in fun and dangerous excitement, than I did. I think I had become too comfortable, even boring to him. Maybe we should have both experienced a little more of life independently before we married. Then he might not feel as if he missed something in his youth. Eventually, his indiscretions were discovered, as one day he brought home more than the milk.

Six weeks of treatment and marriage counseling later, he thought we were back on track as a couple. No way! I was still very angry, so it was my turn to step out on the marriage. I mistakenly believed that I was feeling more anger than pain. After all, it only hurts when I'm breathing. I was determined to experience what I thought he was. The truth is I didn't know what I was looking for and I'm sure I didn't find it.

Revenge is never a good solution to a problem. I found myself pregnant and had to make the hardest decision of my life, to terminate my pregnancy. How could I let myself end up in this predicament is beyond words. He had hurt me, so I wanted to hurt him back. In the end I'm the one who is still hurting, unable to release the guilt, the shame.

What I found stepping out bared no resemblance to my fantasy. It's never as good as the first time. I imagined some fine young thing would sweep me off my feet. We would have a secret hideaway just for us. We would have a "same time next year" story to remember in our golden years. He would lavish me with poetry and presents that I would secretly hide from my husband. There would be poetry that I would memorize and say to myself and then have to explain the unpredictable smile on my face. I was dreaming a made-for-TV movie plot. None of this happened. I need to stop watching *Lifetime*.

I got pregnant from a quickie in the back room of a smoke filled pool hall with a man I barely knew who didn't have two nickels to rub together. Apparently, I thought less of myself than I did of my husband. It has taken a lot of courage, commitment and work to heal myself. Now when I turn off the lights at night, I can finally go to sleep with myself and him. And they lived happily ever after like the folks at "Lake Woe-Be-Gone", Minnesota, where the women are all beautiful and all the children are above average.

# Elaine

## Tears on My Pillow

They say you don't really know a person until you marry them. I'm here to testify that you REALLY don't know a person until you divorce them. You think even though you have problems during the marriage, after the divorce, you can still be "friends". Not in my case. Not in a lot of cases, unfortunately. Jack the jerk was meaner than I ever thought he could be. It was like he morphed into another person. He took out his hostility for me on our young son.

Jack was the one who wanted the divorce in the first place. I can still see the image of my son sitting on the porch waiting on his dad to pick him up after our separation. Eventually, his father remarried and then commenced to treat his first born as though he weren't part of the family. The things they never tell you. During the marriage, my mother in law was treated for depression for years. We thought her hospitalizations were all about back treatments.

Low and behold, my ex husband was also depressed which we didn't discover until he attempted suicide. That I discovered after the divorce. Jack didn't know Jack…and that would be how good he had it with me. Now in hindsight I do recall symptoms, during the marriage, that went unrecognized at the time. Either, I didn't see them or didn't want to see them. Listen, before you marry and have children, check out "grandmas" hidden in the closet. I'm thankful I had enough sense to send my child to a psychologist while he was young. Without it neither of us might have survived his childhood. Today, thankfully, we are both happy and healthy.

# Maryann

## Makin' It Easy for the "Clean Up Woman"

I married young, much too young. And before I knew it, I was the mother of two. I wasn't ready for marriage and children and I knew right away they would suffer from my mistakes. My husband was wonderful, a good man. I had no complaints. Neither of us graduated from college, so he had a mediocre job, except it covered our bills. He kept a roof over our heads and food on the table, which is what a husband should do. I worked part-time to pay for extras. We lived a simple, and good existence.

I watched with envy as my girlfriends went to college, hung out partying, and having a good time. For me, it started slowly and innocently with a girls' night out every once in a while. My husband stayed home with the kids while I recovered a little "me" time. Everything was harmless at first with a smile here, a flirt there. I first started going to clubs without my husband and then parties. What could it hurt? We were just dancing and having a lot of fun.

Before long, I was out of control, way out of control. I was hanging out several nights a week. Why didn't my husband say anything? He didn't complain or even try to stop me. It was too good to be true. I met men, lots of them, some single, some not. I even slept with a few. It didn't mean anything, just making up for some lost youth. Or so I told myself.

I started running into friends, girlfriends, and husbands of friends, at the same parties. This was not a good thing. It didn't matter to me as I always had an excuse why I was "out alone". I was so smart, had everyone fooled. Or so I thought. I was drunk with all the attention I was getting. After all, I was young, attractive and had a great body; good enough to be a model most people used to tell me.

Still do. In retrospect I have discovered everyone knew what time it was, even my husband. My reputation was shot. If you dance to the music, you must be prepared to pay the piper.

Wrapped up in my own life, I wasn't paying attention to my boys or my husband. On a few occasions, my husband and I attended parties together. What a concept! I noticed an inordinate amount of attention he was getting from the other women. Divorced, widowed, single, "available" women were trying to make time with MY man. They had noticed what I had forgotten. He was handsome, hard working and kind. And damn, with me in the streets he was also available! I was making it easy for the clean up woman. It was time for Mustang Sally to get her feet back on the ground.

For the first time in my life, I was terrified. My stomach was in knots. I had always had whatever I wanted and some I didn't want. Now, I was about to lose what I just realized I truly wanted *and* needed, my husband and family.

## I'm Sorry….So Sorry

What was I doing? What was I thinking? I almost lost the best thing that ever happened to me. For days I moped around the house wondering what steps to take; changes to make to turn my husband's head back toward my direction. I think he was beginning to enjoy the attention my so-called friends were showering on him. Their husbands didn't do the dishes, vacuum, or take care of the children. My husband even does my hair, shines my shoes and irons my clothes before I leave.

He had gotten so used to my "bad" behavior, it had become routine, expected. And I took for granted he would always be there for me. I missed a big clue. He didn't smile when I came home anymore. I hadn't even noticed when he stopped.

## Ain't Too Proud to Beg

A simple apology was not good enough. It would never do. I needed to earn back his trust and his love. I put a plan in place and little by little things started to turn around. I stopped the weekend, late night partying cold turkey. What was riding on that midnight train to Georgia was not better than what I had at home. In fact it wasn't even close. Home cooked meals became routine. Cooked by me, that is. My children, growing up rather quickly without me, became my focus. I actually started to enjoy them.

We read stories together, danced to Motown tunes and sat on the front porch, counting cars at night. Instead of just complaining about my life with my husband, we actually started to talk. He actually had dreams too, dreams of owning his own hardware store instead of just working in one. This was something we could work on together. We'd stay up half the night dreaming and planning. We may not get there, but at least we're sharing and talking again.

I'm not too proud to beg and I did. Even, James Brown would be proud of me! It took some time to get our lives back on track, months. But like I said, I married a good man and he's still MY man. Thank the Lord.

# Annie

## He Had a Smile So Sweet...

I met my husband, Calvin, later in life and married later than most of my girlfriends. The way he swept me off my feet, you know he could have been a broom. I was captured by his smile. To me, he was a breath of fresh air, the answer to my prayers. In fact, because most of my life I had felt left out, when I did receive things, I felt truly blessed. I felt blessed when I finished college, got a job, went on vacations and bought a house. So surely, the Lord had sent me this man.

Calvin was intelligent, first in his class at school, had a good job, the sweetest smile and he showered me with gifts. His body was firm and handsome. I thought this is my time. I have died and gone to heaven. The Lord has blessed me again. I used to call him "Sunday Morning".

After two years of marriage, I found out he was more like a "Saturday Night" after too much partying. With the gifts he bought me, he thought he owned me. In his mind, he had bought and paid for me. As time passed, he became more and more abusive, until one day when my three-year-old son observed him attack me with an iron. I knew, if not for my sake, but for my son's, he had to go, sweet smile and all.

## Just My Imagination

The marriage lasted a total of seven years. When I became pregnant, the news was happily received by both of us. Our son was born and we moved into our dream house of four bedrooms with a huge back yard. I imagined that soon they would all be filled with the laughter of children. My imagination turned into a nightmare of reality. At first it was control and possessiveness issues, not physical abuse. We couldn't agree on how to spend time, money or divide up the household tasks.

Saturdays were no longer mine and paired with him, they were no longer productive either. When my husband didn't get his way, he would attack me in some way, sometimes verbally and sometimes physically. I would think about his attacks in order to determine the pattern so as to avoid the abuse in the future. But, I couldn't identify the pattern. Why did this man who professed to love me, hit me? Why did I endure for so long?

When our son was about two years old, I reached a turning point in my marriage. We had just celebrated a wonderful Christmas together. The day after, I expected my husband to return to work as usual. He didn't. He stayed home with us, problem number one. My plans were to do some sewing and clean house. Problem number two. My husband wanted to shop the half price after Christmas sales like his mother always did. I refused, choosing to keep my initial plans, to which he responded by throwing a shoe at me!

I managed to calmly speak with him about this action, which was followed by the usual litany of apologies. I promised myself at that point, that if he ever lost his temper again, I would leave. I tried everything to salvage the marriage and our family. I sought professional help through a therapist who informed me that hitting was Calvin's social tool of management. Somehow I had to find a way to "cure" Calvin as I was pregnant again with our second child.

## Please, Baby Please, Baby Please Don't Go

One crisp October morning, as I sat at the kitchen table grading papers, Calvin walked in and announced that he didn't like the Halloween costume that I made for our son to wear trick or treating. The boy was not yet three, so "what difference does it make?", I said. Big mistake! He threw the iron at me. I was stunned and started to run for cover. Such little provocations could set him off. The next thing I knew, his hands were around my throat choking me. I saw the eyes of a stranger, a man I'd never seen before.

He was like a mad dog foaming at the mouth. His false teeth fell on to my face. Out of the corner of my eye, I could see our son, Matt watching the whole episode. I prayed to the Lord, "If you get me through this, I will never go through it again." When Calvin saw Matt he dropped me like a rag doll. Seeing our son watching in horror must have snapped him back to reality. He began to cry and promised it would never, ever happen again.

"Please don't leave!" "Uh huh"…is all I said to myself. The next morning after he left for work, I packed up what clothes and things I could and headed back home to mom and dad. Over the next thirteen months, we lived a roller coaster ride of an existence. He begged my parents and my sister for my return, refusing to let go of the marriage. Not even a James Brown performance could get me and my child back in his arms. I would never be home alone with him again.

My parents provided the protection we needed and I started to rebuild my life. We bought Calvin out of the house and he moved on to a state of non-existence. His soul continues to be lost, even today, after more than fifteen years have past.

*Sterling and me—making our version of*
*"An Officer and a Gentleman"*

*Our wedding day, August 2, 1969*

*Me and Ster at our 25th anniversary celebration*

*The Park Forest South Fillies*

Chapter Five

# Joy And Pain

*Raising Kids Is Probably The Most Important*
*Thing One Does In Life. It's A Grand Experiment*
*From Start To Finish.*

# Arlene

## Give Me One More Night

Why can't kids be more like pets? My husband and I have now raised two children and four dogs. Let me just admit right now. I think we did better with the dogs. Once they learned you don't "go" in the house, the dogs were no more trouble. Two meals and a couple of walks a day and the dogs are happy. They love and adore us for whatever they receive. Life is just that simple. Why can't kids be like that?

Each day you try and hope for the best, and you don't know for years, if you've actually succeeded. In fact you're never confident you are doing the right thing, making the right decisions. So they will suffer through your mistakes and then through their own. You want them to do better than you have and to make smarter choices. If not better, then at least as well. You try to teach them good values, right from wrong and so on, except they still, whether for good or not, pretty much turn out to be who they were when they got here.

My husband and I never did drugs or smoked cigarettes and seldom indulged in alcoholic beverages, so it was hard for me to understand this temptation for my children. We weren't really tempted. We tried to set the right example when they were young, still do. If your parents were good examples, you try to emulate them right? Like adults, children go through phases too, childhood then adolescence and young adulthood. The outside world can sometimes have more influence on your children than you do. We were stronger and more independent against those forces than our children.

Our children were exposed to music lessons; participated on sports teams; went to camp; were members of Jack & Jill; enjoyed cultural experiences; traveled and volunteered. They were exposed to all of the positive experiences of my childhood and more. We had high hopes and big dreams for their futures. We expected them to advance the ball forward, though right now it doesn't appear that will happen. If only the world stood still, this might work. We need a little more time. Or is it that our dreams don't fit inside their heads. Could it be that they have to paint their own dreams on their life's' canvas?

## Splish Splash

We started our son, Jeffrey, in Montessori school at the age of three. This experience was supposed to provide some structure and discipline in his life, in addition to socialization and early academic learning. A place for everything and everything in its place was the school's mantra. A good start in preschool should produce a good start, we thought, in elementary school.

We started him two hours at a time, moving to half days and then to full days to ease the transition from home and separation from mother. As it turns out, he needed that transition less than I did. From day one, when he saw a room full of other children to play with, he dropped my hand, waved goodbye and said, "See ya, mom." That was it, no tears, no looking back. Other children were tugging at their mother's skirts, crying, begging to go back home. Not my kid. A room full of toys and boys was like heaven to him.

When I came to pick him up, he was never ready to go. "You here already mom?" he would whine. "You must be early." The only time he was upset was when I arrived late and he was the last child to leave. No one likes to be last, I guess. By the end of the day, I could always tell if he had an excellent day by how dirty he was. Those would be his standards, not mine. How does one boy get that dirty in a Montessori school?

Dirt was like a magnet to our son. I could see the other mothers surreptitiously looking at him when I picked him up. I'm sure they assumed that I had brought him to school dirty to begin with, because no one could pick up that much dirt in one day. He needed a bath before dinner. By the way, you can't find that much dirt while reading books or playing with the educational toys either. That was our first clue this kid would never be that interested in academics. And we missed it totally.

## Young Blood

From the moment Jeffrey could see over the opening of the screen door, he wanted to go "outsides, outsides". The weather was never a deterrent. Whether warm, cold, rainy or snowy, he loved the freedom of outside. Jeff would rather wet his pants than come in from playing in the snow. And he did from time to time by waiting until the last minute and not considering the time it would take to remove boots, snowsuit, gloves, hat and scarves. But that was okay, because his second most fun place was splashing in the bathtub and sprinkling cleanser on every available surface in the bathroom.

With few available sidewalks, where we lived, his play was confined to the yard, which was quite large, or the driveway in front of our garage. This confinement on occasion was unacceptable to our "he's all boy" kid. We could never trust him to stay put, whether at home, at the mall or any other place of interest. He was always in exploration mode and on the move. He could drop my hand and disappear in a department store faster than a flea on a dog.

On one occasion, we found him riding his big wheel on the sidewalk that ran parallel to the side of the house. The only way he could possibly have gotten there was to ride in the street, a big NO NO. There he was, staring at us between the slats of the three-foot fence that separated the yard from the sidewalk. From the pensive look on his face, we knew he was working on a good story.

Not wanting to jump to conclusions, we calmly asked how he reached the sidewalk with the big wheel. "Did you ride in the street?" "Oh no", he said, "Jeffrey doesn't go in the street". We asked, "Then how did you get there?". "I lifted my bike over the fence." His dad said, "Let me see you do that again." Jeffrey struggled for ten minutes, trying to lift that big wheel over the fence. Again and again he strained to lift the oversized front wheel over the fence.

With sweat pouring down his stained, red face and teeth gritting, he lifted and pushed to exhaustion. My husband, a man of six feet-six inches in height, who could step over the fence as if it were a mere puddle, reached over the fence, lifting both Jeffrey and the bike with one hand and placed them both on the yard side of the fence.

One swat on the butt sent Jeffrey running to the house with the speed of a silver bullet, which was a good thing. He didn't see us fall to the ground in laughter. He didn't venture from the driveway...you thought I would say "ever again" didn't you? He didn't venture again for two weeks. That was one determined and forgetful kid.

## Where the Boys Are

Our young son was a "player" from the beginning. This use of "player" has nothing to do with women and everything to do with just having a good time. On a summer afternoon, if we couldn't find him, all we needed to do was find a group of boys kicking up dust or throwing rocks. We enrolled him in the usual park district sports programs: baseball, soccer, swimming, tennis and basketball camp, thinking he would take an interest in athletics of some type. He did love going, and it wasn't for the competition or the love of the game. It was just to hang out with the guys.

His eye hand/eye/foot coordination was not the greatest, which never seemed to bother him either. In all those nights, rain or shine, we sat out on dirty benches at dusty baseball fields, I think he hit just one fair ball, maybe two. It never seemed to bother him. He loved sitting on the dugout bench yelling, "Hey batter, batter swing" and rattling the chain link fence. To him, making noise was plenty of fun.

On the soccer field, it didn't matter which end was his team's goal. If he had the ball, he would kick it in any direction. Running and kicking was a lot of fun regardless of which goal the ball went in. For him, the objective of basketball was keep away. We pretended he was somebody else's kid at those games. There was one thing my baby boy could really do well. He could swim like a fish! Only problem was, as parents, we had to sit through hours of swim meets to see him swim a total of about ninety seconds. If you've ever attended a swim meet you are painfully aware of that phenomenon.

## Come See About Me

Our daughter, Pam, has always been the drama queen of the family. In fact, drama is her middle name. She has loved the arts or perhaps being on stage since she could walk and talk. Pam grew up with the entertainment of Janet Jackson and The Blues Brothers. She would spend hours playing both videos, singing and dancing until she knew all the lines by heart. She and her best friend, Leana, would host "shows" in the back yard every summer.

We had a large wooden deck, which served as the stage for their perfor-mances. Days before the event, they would pull a red wagon around the neighborhood passing out flyers detailing the particulars of the next concert. There would be a two-girl *Rhythm Nation Review,* complete with costumes and refreshments. Each event was to be a fundraiser, the profits from which she and Leana would split fifty-fifty.

The expenses were to be split fifty-fifty as well. "Mom do you have any lemon Kool-aid and sugar?" I would make the gallon of lemonade and provide the cooler, cups, ice and napkins. I assumed Leana was bringing the cookies. Just before curtain time, Pam would enter the kitchen again with, "Mom do you have any cookies?" And then it was show time! They were off, Janet and her posse of one, singing their *Rhythm Nation* hearts out. These would not be the first or the last of Pam's drama performances. There were years of school plays and dance recitals. As a result of her dancing lessons, we invested a small fortune in recital costumes, which also doubled as Halloween outfits. That way they were at least worn twice.

In addition to performing in plays, Pam liked writing and telling stories. We used to call her the "bad news" reporter as she always had a long tale of woe about something or someone at school. When most parents ask their children, how was school, they hear the familiar, "Nothing". We, on the other hand, heard a litany of who did what to whom and what happened after that! Once in high school, the stories were replaced with mood swings based on what kind of day she'd had in school that day.

There were days we returned home from work and were afraid to put the key in the door. "You go first." "No, you go in first." We could tell by the look on her face if it had been a good or bad day. At this point she rarely shared the issue that was really bothering her. We would just be on the receiving end of the garbage she was feeling.

I remember on one occasion while in high school, I arranged for Pam to get a hair cut and style at a local beauty shop. She looked Halle Berry gorgeous. The next day at school, she must have looked too good for her evil adolescent girlfriends. Some time during the school day, these girls decided to restyle Pam's hair into a ghetto fabulous do. Admittedly, after spending a fortune on the initial hair style, I was not happy with the reversal when she came home. She wasn't either, and that was never divulged. All we saw was that Pam was angry. And, yep, it was my fault. It was times like these I wished for Elizabeth Montgomery's powers on *Bewitched*, the television show. I could twitch my nose and change the world.

There's still plenty of drama in her life as a young adult, and that of her friends. I get to hear all about it in almost daily phone conversations. She's angry with Rodney, whom she considers to be her boy friend, for dating other women, even though he has made no verbal commitment of monogamy. "But he knows we've been hanging out," she says. That could be any where from two weeks to maybe two months or more. Dating just isn't the way I remember it.

Perhaps these relationships shouldn't even be referred to as dating. I think today it's just called the "hook up". A case in point…TJ, a friend of my daughter, is twenty-seven and seeing two girls, Keesha and LaRonda. LaRonda is only in high school and has no business out until three in the morning. This is where she finds herself as she pursues this unorthodox relationship. Keesha gets mad at TJ for hooking up with LaRonda and slashes his tires. LaRonda calls the police on Keesha as she suspects Keesha of doing the dirty deed. Where is TJ in all of this? Probably moved on to girl number three who has agreed to purchase the needed new tires for his car. And the beat goes on. Sounds like a made-for-TV movie except it's real life, theirs anyway.

## The Words Get In the Way

For years we tried to give our children thoughtful reasons for the life suggestions that we offered them. We believed if they understood the underlying reasons for decisions, it would make sense and result in their cooperation. Eventually in frustration, we would end up saying, "Because I said so". I swore I would never do that. In the end, it was just easier. I tried to teach my daughter financial efficiency, like price comparison-shopping, where to shop, and the advantages of cooking meals at home versus eating out. "Cooking at home may take more time but can result in real savings", I said, and gave several examples.

Regrettably, she continues routinely to eat in fast food restaurants and when she does shop, it's mainly for convenience foods, which are way beyond her meager budget. How does she make ends meet? She shops for groceries and medicines, not at the supermarket, but in her parents' medicine cabinet, pantry and freezer. Sometimes she grocery shops with me as "an outing for the two of us". On these occasions, she will ask me to pick up just a few things that she really needs before payday. Those few things usually fill a shopping cart.

It's easy to tell others what they should do, what direction to take, than it is to actually do it. Telling is easier than doing. "Because I said so" just doesn't work as well as it used to. It's usually followed with, "What'd you say?"

## You Can't Hurry Love, You Just Have to Wait

I think, to our son, we are the Bank of America. This kid has always spent beyond his income, starting with his allowance in junior high school. He even spent all of his high school graduation money during the summer, prior to leaving for college, more than a thousand dollars in two months. That was another behavioral sign my husband and I failed to recognize.

In his early twenties, he would typically max out every credit card in his possession with no consideration for how they would get paid. His mistakes have cost us unnecessary money, stress, and a lot of lost sleep, mostly in areas where we had given guidance that he did not follow. Doesn't he understand how important good credit is? "There are two important things you must maintain", we would tell him: "Your credit and your credibility."

He didn't get it at twenty-one years old; and at thirty, I think he finally does. Of course, now it will take years to regain both from his creditors. Thank goodness, our full employment has been able to maintain him in the life style to which he has become accustomed! Too often our relationship has been one-sided. He needs to understand the importance of mutual support and respect. It's emotionally unhealthy to be hurt and disappointed on a continual basis by anyone, even your own child. Parents have feelings too. We're still waiting for him to show other important signs of maturity. He's thirty-one and counting. This is nothin' like I thought!

## Friends in Low Places

It started with a high level of expectation and high exposure, we thought, to the best things in life, the important things in life and the requirements to be successful in life. We made a deliberate choice to raise our children in an integrated neighborhood. This was no easy task since white folks run out as soon as black folks walk in. The only place integration remained stable during their childhood was at Pilgrimage Church, where the congregation was seriously committed to the importance, beauty and joy of diversity. We exposed them to black children who were both more affluent and less well off than our family, in hopes that they would comfortably maneuver both worlds and have an appreciation for all.

We joined Jack and Jill, a cultural and educational organization for children of color. This organization provided exposure to additional travel, cultural events, an opportunity to meet high achieving students, volunteerism and positive educational and social experiences for our son. No matter what level we aspire for our children, their level of achievement tends to rise no higher than those with whom they spend the majority of their time. Unfortunately, our son aimed rather low. It was easier. Things seemed to move along fairly well until high school. That's when the wheels just fell off the wagon.

Our daughter, whose needs required special services in school, led to classes filled with problem children mainly from a lower economic class. In an attempt to fit in, her values sank deep into the abyss. She was beat down until she no longer felt special. We taught her to accept everyone regardless of their circumstances. They taught her to not accept herself. Her once perfect diction slipped. She prefers long, sometimes blond, fake extensions to her natural hair and fingernails designed beyond description. I tried to follow in my mother's footsteps. She steps everywhere but where mine have been. She now lives in their world and visits mine. Dr. Spock could not begin to address my questions.

"He's all boy", they used to say. I learned later, that comment was no compliment. Play, player, play was Jeff's mantra. Low grades were a goal among his cohorts. Cutting class was a badge of honor. A grade of "D" was OK and a "C" was an exceptional result, worth celebrating! He was ready to head to the Red Lobster for a recognition dinner with every "C" earned. In college, there was no party he couldn't find, whatever the night of the week. His friends tended to have less than he did and to even seek less than he did. This allowed him, we think, to feel like he was "king" of the hill. If you are already at the top of your artificially capped environment, where else would you need to go? He started an uphill climb to the bottom.

We have a second home in Arizona which we hope to use as "snow birds" one day. It has been our son's home rent-free while he finds a better job, a second job; while he finds himself; while he gets himself together; while he does one thing or another for the last four years. It began as another "start over" for him that was to last six months; another strategy for adult growth that has not turned out as planned. I have put him in the Lord's hands a number of times over the years and the Lord keeps giving him back!

## Street Life

Thus far it appears that our children have decided to reject our values, yet I have heard them repeating our advice to their friends. Go figure! Our daughter is forever advising her friends on boyfriends, managing money, living independently. Yet, she herself has yet to choose wisely when it comes to men or manage her money without running short before the next payday. Pam is always the designated driver. This is not because she doesn't drink. She's the only one with a car! We've not yet met one of her boyfriends who has both a job and independent transportation at the same time.

Either they have a job and no car, or a car and no job, or neither. Talk about friends in low places. Unfortunately, they have all been a disappointment to her. I feel her pain except I can't seem to identify a solution for her. These losers are like magnets to her; I believe because she has a kind heart and tries to help those that can't really be helped. Most are just predators taking advantage of her emotional vulnerability.

The steady dose of rap music depicting violence and exploitative, nega-tive representations of women in their videos is counter-productive to a positive self-image as well. From television programming, to radio disk jockeys who "dumb down" their programs to appeal to what they think their audiences want; to movies that exploit the negative side of urban life, there is a subculture defining "blackness" when legitimized by the media as a great influence on our children's lives.

It's a parent's nightmare as we continue to wage battle for the hearts and souls of our children. My brother recently noticed a young teenage black girl in a store with the word "bitch" tattooed on her arm. My daughter even carries a key ring decorated with the saying "I'm not a bitch. I am *the* bitch." Bitch is a negative, derogatory reference to women portraying them as lewd, immoral or generally someone you wouldn't want to be around, much less love.

This word is used over and over in reference to women in rap music. So why would both of these young women refer to themselves that way? Their response is that it's just a word. However, words have power subconsciously and consciously. I would find it hard to believe that a woman who refers to herself as a bitch could hold herself in high regard.

## Daylight and Darkness at the Same Time
Is it the times, the decade, the environment, DNA? I tolerated a lot more attitude from my children than my parents. We understood that adults were in charge. There were boundaries you didn't cross. I remember my mother telling me, "Don't roll your eyes at me!" My kids still don't get it. Did I yell too much and spank too little? Somehow, my parents were able to instill in me, never to do anything that you wouldn't be proud to leave your name on. Your name is important. My children on the other hand, seem to feel any effort is good enough and no behavior is too embarrassing to the family name.

The experiences children have, never really disappear. Sometimes they need help with the interpretation of those experiences. This can be incredibly important if one has chosen to adopt a child.

Both of my children were adopted. We had little knowledge of their lives before coming to live with us. Depending on the age at which you receive your child, he or she may have already experienced abuse, neglect or other negative experiences which can have a large impact on how they handle problems or interpret their future experiences.

These are things that you, as the adopting parent, may never become aware of. Consider that Baby A is planned and being born to loving, excited, expectant parents. The family has prepared a room, a future full of positive expectations. Baby B is perhaps an unplanned or unwanted pregnancy. This child is possibly ignored, did not receive proper prenatal care, and bears the brunt of pain the parents are dealing with. At some point the child is removed from the birth parents, put into the foster system, and is hopefully adopted by loving parents, hopefully sooner than later.

However, this child can be much more needy and insecure. Our daughter was severely neglected as an infant and diagnosed with "failure to thrive" syndrome. She behaved as if she was a deaf child for some time. Through the loving care of a foster family, her senses developed and she became responsive and a more typical three-year-old. She still requires extraordinary emotional support, which I think has its roots in her deprived, early beginning to life. Adoptive parents are rarely trained to deal with the special needs of such a child. Love is not enough.

## Purple Rain

How does your garden grow? Weeds don't need rain or sunshine. They just seem to grow with or without intervention. Initially we have really high expectations and aspirations, when our children are preschoolers. To most parents, their children are seen as gifted and talented in everything they do. I could barely drive into the garage from work before the kids would pounce on me with news of the day, what happened at preschool. They were always excited meeting me at the car door. "Watch me do this or that." "I need a new something for school."

After they started real school, and somewhere around Junior High, I just hoped they would pass, and by High School, just get through the year with this or that teacher. Next, I hoped they would at least graduate high school. Then whether they attended college or not, I hoped they wouldn't do drugs, go to jail, have children until married, in short, stay away from the "pipe and the pole" as Chris Rock would say. Eventually, I lowered the expectations to, "Can we all just get along?"

I don't want them to be a fool or be played for a fool. I expect my children to contribute to this world. I would hope that they would be able to work in a job they enjoy, pay their taxes, not just vote, but passionately engage in the political process and give back to their community; somehow, perhaps through volunteerism. This is the example I have set except I don't expect that my footsteps will be followed. There ought to be a class in how to raise children, except who do you know that is qualified to teach it? Unfortunately children don't come with a set of instructions, nor a guarantee.

They say young people today grow up too fast. Each generation of children seems to enter adulthood earlier. I say it seems they'll never grow up. True, they are exposed to adult issues and life far too soon. They seem incapable of assuming adult responsibilities until well into their thirties, if then. For example, they are exposed to sex and lots of it at the movies and on television; however, they ignore the importance of safe sex and birth control. They certainly are not ready for the responsibility of parenting, as they have no clue as to how much money, time, sacrifice, patience and energy raising children takes. Can we get flowers to grow among the weeds?

## Town Without Pity

The lies we tell. Don't you just hate hearing your friends bragging about how wonderful and perfect their children are? I found this really depressing until I figured out they were lying. Parents lie. I don't blame them. I thought I was all alone with the two numb-skulls we were trying to raise, until one other parent confided in me, the problems she was also experiencing. What a comfort. Just think how much we could have helped each other were it not for all the pride or rather false pride. Really, THEY DON'T KNOW JACK EITHER!

It's easy to pretend for a short time that things are different and problems don't exist. It helps to know you are not alone. Most often, parents don't mean to lie. They are just telling the story the way they want it to be. I can relate to that.

## If It Takes All Day, If It Takes All Night...

As parents, are you ever through raising kids? Or is it like weeding the garden, never finished! Gee, I don't think our parents felt this way while we were growing up! Or did they? I think it's all relative to the decade of your teenage years. Decades do make a difference. I'm a child of the sixties; a time of questioning values; challenging politics; saving the world; marching for Civil Rights. It was a time when we accepted individual differences and even celebrated them, fought for them. In the decades following the sixties, society has become much more "me" centered. What have you done for me lately? What's in it for me? I don't care what you want; this is MY LIFE.

We are now at a point where many of our children have grown up comfortably and seem to take it for granted. They don't remember the blood, sweat and tears it took to get to this place. They've forgotten or never really learned *their* history. Financial success is a right of passage for which the debt of hard work and effort has been paid by the parents and those that have gone before. Each genera-tion that preceded had to endure the pain and suffering of discrimination, lost opportunities; accepting menial jobs to feed the family and keep a roof overhead. Their very lives were threat-ened for minor infractions of status quo, like looking too closely at a white woman or trying to vote.

Whatever it takes to get ahead we were willing to do, no matter what the effort or the sacrifice. This internal drive for excellence, I've found, has been difficult to transfer to a new generation removed ever so slightly from the not so distant past.

## Mama Didn't Lie

If only love were enough. Let me repeat, life is all about choices. You try to teach your children so they make the right choices (those we think are right anyway). Yet they can make really poor choices anyway and no matter how hard you try to spare them the pain, they just have to go there anyway. There is no promise of easy street. I've learned kids will live their own lives and you have to let them, no matter how poorly they make choices.

I decided to talk to other mothers honestly about my children, sharing what they were doing that drove me crazy. Sometimes they had really good ideas I hadn't considered. At any rate, it helped me to know that I was not alone. Those newsletters in the Christmas cards do not always reveal the whole truth. You may even discover you're not as bad off as you thought. I did. It may be surprising, but there are kids worse than yours! It's hard for kids to meet all their parent's expectations. Mine aren't really so bad. No matter what they become or where they end up in life, I will always love them.

# Cynthia

## California Dreamin'

Who, me, worry? I have two great kids whose reality has never quite been my reality. They think money grows on trees. Success will always come. They have gourmet tastes and think a McDonald's budget will cover it. They don't worry about anything; for in their world everything is gonna work out fine. They both graduated from high school with athletic scholarships, which they lost after their freshman years. This put a serious crunch on my husband's and my budget, and yet they never seemed to feel it. Everything is gonna work out fine.

They don't worry about minor things, like checking the oil before taking a road trip; paying parking tickets and credit cards on time; submitting the proper forms before graduation so your name appears in the program; driving with a license.

Once, my sons and a friend took a road trip to Florida for spring break. They're big boys now so I tried not to be apprehensive. Thankfully, they decided to spend the night in Atlanta with my brother along the way. Praise God for brothers and uncles. They got a good night's rest and before they left, he asked if they had checked the oil recently. "Ahh, I don't think so Uncle Jim." They pulled the dipstick out and stared at it with a puzzled look on their faces.

In and out again with the dipstick. It was as dry as desert sand. Like I said, it's gonna work out fine. As bright as they are, they could never keep up with little things like hats, gloves, coats and scarves in the winter. How do you forget your coat when it's cold outside? They never forgot a practice or a ball game. Isn't it funny how that works out. It's gonna be just fine.

# Elaine

## Doing the Best We Can

I don't think I had a good parenting model. My parents were much older, in their forties, when I was born. They were more like my grandparents. I had no idea what raising a child would be like. When I married I thought things would be different, more exciting, at least more fun. So I married and had a child. My son was a difficult baby and sickly his first two years. He was very intelligent, but a real handful. Even my teacher training didn't help at the times. My parents were no help and my husband was completely useless. He couldn't even change the diapers without gagging.

When our son was two and a half we divorced. Dr. Spock and I did the best we could. It turns out my best was good enough. My son has an education, a job, a wife, and is very happy. I think I will be able to depend on him in my old age. Now that's how it should be.

# Linda

## I've Been Searching

My mother always told me, "You are who your friends are." So I passed these words of wisdom on to my daughter. There was just one problem. Nice girls just weren't "nice" to my daughter. My daughter is special. Born to me later in life, she was like an only child, as her brother was much older. She is kind hearted, physically attractive, a rather sensitive and giving person.

She also has special needs academically which meant she couldn't always keep up with the interests and conversations of the more academically talented. The academically talented were also defined as the nice girls, considered to be well brought up with good manners, goals and bright futures. She was soundly rejected by these "nice" girls, which left her to choose from a handful of friends in her special education classes.

The girls in her classes tended to be rough around the edges, from dysfunctional homes and in need of counseling due to emotional and behavioral problems. Some were just plain old mean, not that "nice" girls aren't also mean. They formed groups whose only purpose was to exclude others. The excluded ones formed groups to further exclude. By default, this left my daughter between a rock and a hard place, ridiculed by those with less for being too middle class and ignored or shunned by others who had little understanding or patience for her uniqueness.

I've been searching for a middle ground somewhere. Is there a teenage daughter somewhere with empathy and compassion for others? Empathy and compassion in the same sentence as teenager is probably an oxymoron. Has anybody seen JACK?

# Mavis

## Call Me, I'll Be There

When it comes to raising children, instinct helps. Do what you think is right and it still may not turn out the way you hope. I decided to stick to basic rules.

Things, I wish I'd known:

1) How to be more accepting of a child's assets and not what I thought they should be.

2) It is OK to not know everything. You can find some answers together. No matter how hard you try, adults don't always have all the answers for their children.

3) Kids have dreams that sometimes aren't realistic. And you have to let them try even if they fail. For example, maybe the dream of dental school is not going to work out. You, as the parent, are already aware of this fact. The academics are much more difficult than your child can handle; however, being a dental assistant is a possible option. You have to work together toward that realization or the child will think you withheld opportunity from him or her. Losing the dream will forever be your fault.

## It's The Same Old Song

I've learned that it is all right to be <u>RIGHT</u> where you are at the moment. It is fruitless trying to put a square peg into a round hole. I buried my feelings, whatever they were, instead of responding and dealing with them. It's always more painful in the long run to ignore them. I've recently become a grandmother. I thought I would be a mother-in-law first and I'm still waiting for that role to materialize.

Kids today don't seem to adhere to the rules by which we functioned under penalty of death. At least, we thought our parents would kill us if we broke them. Like sex before marriage! We'll never know because we didn't test the rules. We blindly obeyed. My grandchild is beautiful and I love her. As with most things, eventually this will all work out too. At least I will do my part. Still, a good rule to remember…if you can't say something nice, don't say anything. So we will work it out and I will do my best to avoid the taste of shoe leather.

# Annie

## Money Don't Bring Everything it's True

Affluence does not bring good things, necessarily. Many of my friends' children live in neighborhoods with large homes where there are no sidewalks and very little public transportation. This means the kids are either driven to school by mom, or they take a bus. Here is what they miss. My friends and I walked to and from school, every day, and sometimes home for lunch. Not only was it good exercise, but we communicated with each other. We developed long and lasting relationships through these talks on our walks.

We learned what we had in common, likes and dislikes, shared ideas on homework, solved sibling disagreements and generally bonded in a way you can't do on a noisy bus. We took different routes occasionally to "explore" new blocks in the neighborhood. Sometimes, we explored new routes just to prolong the walk and our conversation. Often when we arrived at one of our homes, we would sit on the porch and watch the cars go by. We each took a color and counted the cars as they whizzed by. Whoever had the largest count at the end of our time together, we imagined would own the car of her dreams.

Sometimes we just sat and picked out pictures of outfits in the Sears catalog. We imagined ourselves dressed in these pretty outfits at parties or wherever our imaginations took us. There were no winners or losers in these games. Anyone could play and she didn't need to be tall, strong, slim, smart, wealthy or pretty, just friendly.

# Denise

## A Real Mother For Ya

We raised our children to be independent thinkers, so I don't know why my husband and I have been surprised by their ensuing independent behavior. I enjoyed motherhood, though things didn't turn out the way I expected. We raised our children not to feel out of place anywhere. And as Martha Stewart would say, "That's a good thing".

Since my husband and I had both attended nearly all white, Eastern colleges and felt very much out of place, we did not want that isolating experience for our children. After all, they should be successful, strong, confident adults in every culture, right? How else will you be able to hold your own in corporate America? My son works hard, is a good husband and family man. I'm very proud of him.

He married outside our African American culture, and that's my issue. It's not that I have anything against white people. I just think successful black men should marry successful black women and continue to uplift the race. Initially, I felt when one considers from whence we have come; slavery, legalized segregation, oppression, lynchings (the first terrorists); and economic exploitation, marrying white some how seems like you are turning your back on the struggle. You are forgetting the past and rejecting who you are.

I forget sometimes that people can just love each other despite the past and the baggage it brings with it. The kids love each other and I did raise him with an open mind. So there you go. My daughter is bright and extremely creative working in the arts. She's a strong woman who knows herself and exactly what she wants. At thirty, she announced to her father and me that she was gay. I spent a total of five minutes asking myself, "How did this happen?", "Was it something I did or said?" Clearly at the end of my brief, internal discussion with myself, "I already knew that!" This was a fact that had been obvious to us for some time. And yes, we will still love her tomorrow!

*Pam and Jeffrey before the influence of the outside world*

*The kids enjoying their new puppy*

*Our "all boy" son seeing the bright side of everything*

*The drama queen at age 7*

*Pam and Jeff graduation, June 1993*

Chapter Six

# The Big Five-O

*We Had All The Time In The World....*
*Where Did It Go?*

# Arlene

## Dancing in the Street

Life, in my twenties, was good times that flew by incredibly fast. I had unbelievable amounts of energy, could play sports and not feel it the next day, and eat whatever I wanted. And I do mean whatever! I used to eat Bosco (remember that?) with a spoon from the jar. Ready Whip in an aerosol can, aimed in the mouth, went directly down the throat. I didn't need a piece of pie to justify a scoop of ice cream.

Twenty-somethings can burn calories just sitting in a chair and thinking, which actually is the point. In your twenties you are never sitting and thinking. I was always on the move! Running here and there, dancing the night away, playing sports, hiking, being all I could be and then some.

In your twenties, you finally have independence, except do you really have any sense? I thought I did. Success was very important, mainly defined by financial evidence. This was important to me, my spouse, friends and everyone's parents. I was still obsessed with making all those people from my childhood proud of me, worth all their efforts. After all, old folks need to have young folks they can point out and say how they "knew them when". That's such a fun game to play as you age. I'm now a player. The game starts by saying "I remember thirty years ago…" I never thought this decade would pass so quickly.

## Rock Around the Clock

The thirties brought the children and I finally had to figure out the responsibility thing once and for all. Not that I hadn't always been a sensible and responsible person, I now completely understood that I was on my own and others now depended on me. I was independent of my parents as I was now a parent. The thirties came so quickly, I felt I must do all the things I thought I would have accomplished before turning thirty, like tap dance lessons, that masters degree, horseback riding, owning a business. It was OK because the kids were small and could go wherever I went. So I enrolled in a lot of silly classes trying to catch up with my so-called life.

## If We Could Start Anew I Wouldn't Hesitate

Toward the end of the forties the waiting game began: Waiting for the kids to graduate college so we could reclaim our income. Waiting for the kids to get a job and pay their own bills. Waiting for the kids to "grow up". Waiting for them to get married. Waiting for the grandchildren to come along so we could spoil them and send them home. I'm still waiting: Waiting for the freedom to reinvent myself. Waiting for the magic age when I can finally retire from that job that lately hasn't been all that!

## A Change is Gonna Come

Turning fifty…our second adulthood, is the best of all times. How did I end up here so quickly? Feels like it only took five minutes! Over the hill at fifty, sliding right down toward sixty, to grandmother's house we go? Grandmother's house we become. What hill is that, anyway, that people say you're over? Most of us are still where we were. Same job, same bills, same life…looking for a hill to conquer.

In your fifties, you have reduced energy, but more money to travel in style. I wouldn't go back for anything, except thirty-two was a very good year. Though now at fifty plus, somehow, I can't remember exactly why. Could it be that it was a time that I looked really, really good, like firm and slim? My mother warned me that each decade would bring something new and interesting, but not always pretty. I'm fifty pounds heavier than the weight I swore I'd never be. Exercising, which was once part of my lifestyle, is now a major chore. I haven't given up. I'm working my way back to some resemblance of me! It will never be the same and that's all right.

My choices have gotten more practical, like whether to eat that box of Girl Scout thin mint cookies or just walk on by. "Well", I say to myself, "they only become available once a year and the Girl Scouts do need the money". So what could one box hurt, maybe two. Actually my favorite poison is double chocolate fudge brownies. I prefer to think of chocolate as one of the basic food groups. It should be. For me, it's medicinal.

Why is it when you ride a bike at eight you burn more calories than when you're fifty? Did you know that as you get older your body stores more sugar as fat, especially in the abdomen and upper body? Yes, girlfriends, that's where that characteristic "pouch" comes from. When I sit down, I feel my belly pushing up against my bra and resting on my thighs at the same time. Damn, when did I eat that much? I've learned my body has becomes less sensitive to insulin, which moves fat and sugar. The blood sugar stays a little higher than normal after meals, which as we age, seems to be more important to us than before.

Only old folks think three meals a day are important, especially breakfast. We learned that growing up in health class. And left over pizza is not an appropriate menu for breakfast! So we eat a full meal; bacon, eggs, grits or hash browns, toast, maybe fruit, juice and coffee. That would be coffee with cream, real cream. The fix, of course, is diet *and* exercise.

The thought of diet and exercise is certainly what I look forward to everyday when I rise. My doctor just suggested I count my calorie intake for the next two weeks. This would increase my awareness of how many calories I really do eat. Like that would be a surprise to me. Less is more. Time to "tighten up"!

## I Feel Like Bustin' Loose

Fifty would be perfect were it not for menopause and "Personal Summers". Is menopause payback for the Garden of Eden? We must have done something wrong at some point! Is the heat on? I used to be cold all the time, especially my hands and feet. I affectionately called my husband the "radiator" and he used to keep me warm at night. Sadly, I don't need that any more. I can be his radiator.

I used to sleep in flannel pajamas. Now even nude, I'm not cool enough. I could sleep with air conditioning in the winter! When that heat surges up my spine, it feels like aliens have invaded my body. I have found that if I stick one foot from under the covers it actually helps. Go figure! A glass of cold water helps too, except it causes those middle of the night trips to the bathroom.

My husband says he's going through menopause with me. When I get hot, he gets hot. Please. What does he know? It's on and off with the covers all night long. He has to eat what I eat, except, he's not allowed near my chocolate. A person could get hurt doing that. When I can't sleep, it wakes him up too. Of course it doesn't count when his snoring wakes me up. When you live with someone you somewhat go through what they experience, the mood swings, hot flashes, night sweats, insomnia. That's what he thinks! As dear as he is, he doesn't know JACK either.

When it comes to being a woman, men are clueless. They can develop an appreciation, but they can never know what it's like to have a period, give birth or what it means to go through the "change". Personally I'd like to ex"change" that for something else, please.

## Ain't That a Bitch

He called me ma'am as he helped me empty the grocery cart. Ma'am? This is not the south, so it is not a common courtesy to say ma'am and sir. I asked my girlfriend if I looked *that* old. Her answer was a little too honest for my fragile ego that day. "You look like a middle-aged woman." Her response was meant as a compliment, "You know, *good* for your age." It was never the less a reality check. I have "crossed over".

We start out telling our age with the exactness of year and month. "I'm six and a half", we say with pride. Then we look forward to being sixteen and able to drive the car. We lie trying to pass for twenty-one. Some time around thirty or forty, we become self-conscious about age. At fifty we are aware of our own mortality, especially as friends and classmates begin to die too soon from one ailment or another. Frankly it's not death that worries me the most. I'm not afraid to die. I'm afraid to be dependent on our health care system in America.

Insurance companies tell doctors what they can do and how well they can care for you. They determine if you can receive the surgery or medications needed. And I don't want to end up in a nursing home on drugs to keep me quiet and easy to ignore. So, although, I plan to take good care of myself, I also plan to have a good time while I can. Where's the chocolate?

## There Goes My Baby

One really good thing about turning fifty…You are finally free of homework and the kids' schedules. That's if you didn't start your family late, or worse yet, start over again after a divorce, or even worse yet, are raising your grandchildren. Having babies in your forties may not be too painful. Having teens in your fifties or sixties? Now that's a pain. Chances are you may have to work way beyond what you planned to support the college tuition of the future.

I pray for my girlfriends who are full-time grandmothers raising adolescent girls today. With the advent of the cell phone and Internet, it's harder to stay on top of what they can get themselves involved in. It was easier when you could find notes in their pockets while doing the laundry. Those notes revealed a great deal of information as conversation starters that still left them wondering, "How did you know that?"

By fifty, our kids were finally gone. Well that's because in a way, we paid them to leave. My kids wouldn't leave the nest. It was too comfortable for them. We "helped" them leave. We, on the other hand, had to move from our parent's home to enjoy real freedom. Conversely, our kids had a lot more freedom growing up than we ever did, right at home. Their world was a lot bigger than ours. We walked or took the bus wherever we went, which limited the distances and times we traveled. They had their own cars and traveled places that we parents are still learning about over casual Thanksgiving dinner conversation.

We abstained out of fear of pregnancy. They had birth control readily available to them. We had limited access to alcohol depending on the virtues of older friends. They had access to technology to make near perfect replications of IDs that could get them anything they wanted from the adult world. So why leave home? It wasn't necessary.

Our kids enjoyed plenty of freedom and had lots of money to spend, as they did not assist with any of the household bills. However, when the elderly and or ill parents started to move in, that was just too many generations under one roof! So we paid the down payment for our daughter's condo to assist in her moving out. We allowed our son to temporarily move into our second home in Arizona. Two years later, we had to assist with the move out of that home by paying three months rent in "his" apartment as start up help. That led to another three months when threatened with eviction.

Now, he's thirty and just beginning to see the light of maturity. Today, they are both still periodically on the "payroll" so to speak; short on that next payment due; need a little gas money, and hungry.

I'm beginning to wonder if my kids will marry and have children and return the favor of driving them crazy. Over the past twenty-five years, I've bought an immeasurable amount of gradua-tion gifts and countless wedding and baby shower gifts for the children of our friends. At Pam and Jeff's current rate of activity, I'll be dead or on a walker by the time our friends can return the favor. Maybe I should throw a "I'm broke again and my mom and dad are tired of picking up the slack so can you help a brotha and sista out shower" for the two of them.

Life is what happens while you're making other plans. You did have a plan, didn't you? I thought I had a plan. I planned to marry, have two children, become a famous writer and retire at fifty, living a life of leisure. I changed it and it changed me. Mostly I let it slip by while addressing the necessities of daily living.

## And the Beat Goes On

At fifty, we hopefully no longer feel the need to "prove" ourselves at work. They know we have skills because we finally believe it too. We can take more risks. Sadly, we are quite possibly also considered dinosaurs. We've been around too long and know too much history. Ordinarily that could be considered an asset. In today's fast paced world, history is the last quarter. If your head goes back too many quarters and you remember how things used to be done, it can be a liability, especially when management is trying to pass off a process as "new" that we old heads have certainly done before.

Sales plans go full circle on a regular basis. One year we were paid for revenue only despite the product sold; the next on revenue and profit; the next on categories of revenue (i.e. software, PCs, services, servers, etc.) and then back to revenue only for whatever product and services sold, and revenue and profit.

The bean counters just can't seem to get the mix right. The mix is whatever pays the sales representative the least without making them feel they have no chance of making the quota number. There must always be some measure of hope. We have to be able to bend whichever way the wind blows. I wish I were a willow and then at times I wish I were a mountain. Strong enough to take whatever is thrown at me.

Now, at fifty, we're starting to gray around the temples and we need glasses to read the fine print. So what! I've got fat under my arms, but not in my head. I faithfully never stopped learning something new. I have finally learned that as soon as I learn the rules, the rules change, so I make up my own rules! Confidence is everything. I'm over fifty and still trying to figure out what I want to be when I grow up. I've had several careers, each of which has brought both excitement and boredom. I'm ready for whatever comes next.

## High Hopes

Now is the time when many people start to look backward. There's more *lifetime* in the past than forward in the future at this point. The oldies on the radio are newer than what I danced to in high school. So what is my music, really old oldies? I refuse to get stuck in the past with regrets or changes I wish I had made. This is not the end of my usefulness. I'm not obsessed with youth. I'd rather be me than them just starting to go where I've already been. When it's over, it's done. Finished!

I actually have more freedom to do what I want after the age of fifty than before. My plan is to embrace aging with style and grace, as my mother did. She accepted the changes and adjusted her life to them. My "change of life" will be a reinventing of myself. At present, my life has more or less accelerated. I need to move with some speed before it's time for assisted living! It's not too late to chase a dream or two. I'm not checking out in a rocking chair or catching dust on a shelf.

I have decided to take the risk. At this moment, I have little to lose so, I'm writing this book. A dream I've held for years. Maybe it will be a best seller, or maybe it won't. If it isn't, maybe I'll take up pottery. What means the most is that I did it. I finally did it! Are you feeling me girlfriends?

## Working My Way Back to YOU

I am becoming my mother. I see her in my hands, my hips, my neck. Her voice even comes out of my mouth. Of course, this started happening long ago, and now I recognize it, accept it, even welcome it. After all, she's been my role model, my mentor, my friend…ever since I figured out she wasn't the enemy. Mothers have many words of wisdom that become more meaningful as you age. My daughter is just beginning to figure this out. Now in her twenties, there are days when she doesn't hear a word I say and then days she calls me four or five times just to ask my opinion.

Unfortunately, outside influences (i.e., stupid inexperienced friends still carry a great deal of weight on decision-making, contributing to errors in judgment). I pray these errors in judgment will be less and less of a financial burden for us as parents. Are we forever doomed to lifting the kids out of the holes they dig for themselves?

Sometimes I miss those days of yesterday, high school, college, early marriage, young children. I miss my mother. I'm not depressed about becoming older yet I can't quite accept that more than half a century has passed before my eyes. I used to feel a sense of urgency to get everything done. I still get things done but with less self-imposed stress. I am more relaxed and at peace, comfortable in my zone. I am not young, yet I am not old. I am like a puzzle with no missing pieces.

## I'll be Dog Gone

Speaking of parents, if you are blessed to have them for a long time, well past eighty, be prepared to take over their lives. *Be Prepared*. You won't always see it coming, one day if you're lucky, they just turn it over to you. My mother did. Shortly after she moved into senior apartment living, she handed me her checkbook, her prescriptions, a list of things she needed and that was it. Fortunately, my own life was in good order before this happened. I could assume the burden in an orderly fashion. When that ball gets tossed, you have to be in position to catch it and hold on. The key is organization.

My parents did really well for a long time. My father passed away at the tender age of seventy six and mom carried on fairly well until the age of eighty. Despite the affliction of Parkinson's disease, she aged beautifully. There was never a fight about downsizing, when it was time to stop driving or anything of the usual issues elder care can bring. She made all those decisions for herself, which my sister, brother and I then carried out on her behalf. It did surprise me though, the day she basically turned her life over to me.

Mom had moved to senior apartment complex. Her health and physical dexterity were beginning to fail. Her once beautiful handwriting was barely legible. Little by little, she had assigned tasks to us like power of attorney for health and finances. Our names were on various bank accounts and CDs. She moved ten minutes away from me, into the senior living complex and then she just did it. She turned everything over to me, the decisions, paying of the bills, dispensing of medication, shopping, transportation to wherever she wanted to go.

I became the parent. It was an interesting but not unmanageable juggling act. Like I said, you need to be organized. We had a lot of fun together. Then one day, just when I had it all figured out, all in proper balance, I lost her. No matter what your relationship has been with your parents, be it good or bad, close or distant, when they're gone, you really miss them.

I really, really miss both of my parents. My dining table seems less full at holiday time without them, even when we invite extra guests in an attempt to make up the difference. And there are so many times I want to ask a question, share a thought, idea, funny story with them. It would be so nice to just pick up the phone.

## Three Times a Lady

"The lady crossed her legs and crossed over." At my mother's funeral, the minister said she was first and last a "lady". This was a fine description of my mother. Growing up, she emphasized in many ways how important it was to always remain a "lady". It was important to set a correct table whether for a full meal or a snack. Grammar was to be impeccable. This was one reason we were never allowed to watch the *Amos and Andy* TV show which exaggerated black culture and people.

Amos, his wife Saphire and Andy were forever using poor grammar and making ignorant decisions. We were not allowed to swear, not even to use substitute swear words like, "oh fudge" for "oh shit", "heck" for "hell", or "dang" for "damn". The intent was still the same she would say. We would get sent to our rooms for calling each other stupid. Sit up straight, cross your legs at your ankles, tuck in your blouse and the really big one...You don't ever call boys. They should call you!

This was how I began to suspect that my mother was deteriorating in her final days. She easily said things that in years passed would never have been said in the company of others. A friend bought her a box of chocolates for Valentine's Day. Instead of the usual, "Thank you, they taste wonderful," or something to that effect. She said, "These look like cheap chocolates from the drug store." Thank goodness the thoughtful gift bringer had already left the premises.

Mom was in the hospital two weeks before she passed away. Late one evening as we discussed her impending return to the senior citizens complex where she resided, I mentioned how glad her dinner partners would be to see her again. She gazed at me with a curious look in her eye and said, "I wonder if Rose is still wearing that simple wig cocked sideways on her head." Old folks have a tendency to tell the truth as they see it whether it is polite or not. That can get sticky in public places. These were very much out of character statements from a woman who would rather die that say an unkind or impolite word to anyone. A slight exaggeration of course, but she was losing all decorum.

After she passed away and my sister and I were going through her things, we found a hamper filled with purses. There must have been two or three dozen different purses of all sizes, colors, styles, some plain leather, some beaded or covered with colorful sequins. In each purse we found: a small comb, package of tissues, throat lozenges; often a tube of lipstick and pocket change. The lady was never without her purse and the basic necessities.

## Feel the Need

My parents died too soon, gracefully exempting me and my siblings of much of the experience of elder care that my husband is now traveling through. His father has been diagnosed with dementia for several years and what an exciting progression that has been. When your elderly parents live in another state, there are signs of trouble you miss because they are not evident in short visits or phone conversations.

Initially grandpa was paying bills twice or not at all. And then there were the caregivers who would routinely escort him to the bank for daily withdrawals, which landed in their pockets, not his. He's a walking history book of events and people twenty years ago, but can't remember a conversation ten minutes ago. He sometimes thinks the first wife is the second one, which makes for an interesting visit.

Once there was a spring trip from Ohio to Florida in his camper, which ended in a stay at a Charter Hospital, after he was picked up by the Orlando police while "lost" in a parking lot. The police called my husband to recover his father where upon his arrival at the hospital, grandpa asked, "You staying at this hotel too?"

My husband drove grandpa to Arizona to stay with relatives, only to have him show up at Midway airport in Chicago two days later; escaped again. "I need my clothes and my car," he said. That was the first of several trips my husband would take to retrieve his "lost" father until we moved him to our hometown for safe keeping. This is the merry-go-round for some in elder care of lost and found; hospital to rehab and back; to home care and back to hospital; rehab and finally, hospice.

# Cynthia

## Wake Up Little Susie

The AARP card came in the mail today. That can only mean one thing, DISCOUNTS! Yea! My husband's card came a year ago, and he threw his in the trash. AARP to him represented all the career disappointments, unrealized accomplishments, and finite existence that comes with being the big five 0. Not for me. I signed up for both of us and dropped that puppy in the mail. After all I was in the height of my career. Fancy title, great income, stock options, fabulous perks. I had it all. Then just like the Chicago Bulls campaign, everything changed.

Everything can change in the blink of an eye. Everything can change in the blink of an eye! EVERYTHING CAN CHANGE IN THE BLINK OF AN EYE! The job is gone. The new business is a bust. The 401Ks have been depleted. My mom's inheritance sucked into the same "black hole" and I owe money to my sister and brother-in-law. DAMN!

Fifty reminds me of the highs and lows of my twenties. I was a happy go lucky college student, an elementary school teacher extremely active in my union, and a new bride by age twenty-three. Then life happened. You know, the stuff that happens while you're making other plans. By the time I hit thirty, I had divorced and remarried, changed my career path and had my first mortgage. OH! And I owned my first convertible, a TR6 complete with British flag painted on the rear side. I was so cool! BUT, here I sit at fifty, totally broke for the second time in my life with lessons not learned.

We've reneged on all the travel invitations we received this year, except with my sister. I never seem to be able to say "no" to her and actually stick with it. As a matter of fact, I said no to this chapter, "noooo" to this taped interview last Saturday. Here I am talking into her tape recorder and emailing a transcript to make the transcribing easier. But, then, that's what being a girlfriend is all about.

## Am I the Same Girl?

Growing older and growing "out" was something that was not supposed to happen to me. I grew up watching my overweight aunts leaving no prisoners at the holiday dinner table thinking that would never happen to me. Yet, here I sit, one hundred pounds above my high school cheerleading weight with a mug of chocolate pudding in one hand, a spoon in the other and a puzzled look on my face asking myself what happened! Let me tell you about a game my Aunt Sis and a friend used to play called "keeping it even, keeping it real". It doesn't matter what you are eating, whether meat and potatoes, or dessert.

During dessert, however, is when it's played most frequently. You have something like pie and ice cream on your plate. If you run out of ice cream before the pie, then you add a little ice cream to go with the pie. If you run out of pie and still have ice cream, then you add pie. See this game can go on forever keeping it "even" until the ice cream and pie are completely gone. And that's how you start to lose that cheerleading figure. Keeping it even and keeping it real....real chocolate, real butter, real whipping cream, real sugar, real Smithfield's ham. Get it? No substitutions! It's in my DNA. That's my story and I'm sticking to it. Am I the same girl? Yes I am. Yes I am.

## Because I am a Queen

Evidently, I'm not alone because all of my aunts, and that would be on both sides of my family, are life time shoppers at Lane Bryant's department store, a store for big women, sizes eighteen plus. I started as a size eight then moved up annually until I reached a size fourteen. This I could live with until one day the sales person suggested a fourteen W. "W", what's a W?

I learned a W meant wide. It made room for my ever-widening chest, which didn't quite need a sixteen yet; and a little more length to make up for the additional lift, from the ever-widening chest. It was like someone stuck a hose in me started blowing me up and out. I don't shop Lane Bryant like my aunts. I have options today of any department store so long as they have a Women's section.

Doesn't Women's section sound better than plus sizes? I once knew a store called Ladies at Large. Who thought that marketing plan would be successful? We've come a long way from full-figured bras, to Ladies at Large boutiques; to Just My Size panty hose; to Curves Fitness Centers in the new millennium. That's the gym where "my people" go who don't want to work out in sweats next to the skinny one in spandex at the health clubs. However, this is the year I'm "really" going to drop fifty!

Right now I'm up one, but it's muscle weight. The trainer at the club has a routine worked out for me that begins with a ten-minute warm up on the life cycle. The life cycle gives me added weight loss benefit like the old Gloria Marshall reduction salons that would roller beat the fat out of you. The concept was, break down the fat and flush it out. Well, with each revolution on my life cycle, my knees are beating the fat out of my belly. I wish! It's time to downsize and I'm not talking about the house.

# Annie

## Voice Your Choice

I had planned milestones for my life. By the age of thirty, I would have a house, finish my master's degree, go to Europe, and be married. By forty, I would have three or four children and be madly saving to send the little geniuses to college. I would also be climbing the ladder of success at my job and making more money. By fifty I would retire comfortably and travel the world. Those things did not happen in my planned time frame or in the planned order. Some didn't happen at all.

In my twenties, I was a "material girl" with her sights on everything beautiful and wonderful. I couldn't find a blouse I liked unless it came from Neiman Marcus. I thought I needed to make up for a childhood absent of material possessions. I had to reject my mother's ideas of finance, that being, buy everything on the cheap. As well, I rejected her religious life, which I saw as too confining while I was trying to find myself and figure out how to survive.

So I traveled, bought my house and generally lived the good life. I discovered a house was not always a physical place. It was more like a life that you build from the bottom up and out, brick by brick. I did marry in my thirties, but by forty I was a single parent trying to hold on to my house and save enough to send my one child to college. Now that I think about it, I couldn't have handled more children. They take a great deal more energy and planning than I anticipated. I did retire at fifty-nine with a new definition of comfort. I now know that I can live with a lot less materially. This will be an "0" year. That means I'm turning sixty (60), another milestone. I have no milestone planned for this decade other than to be healthy and happy. I think that's plenty.

# Denise

## Gee Whiz

I have to admit, my life has turned out the way I wanted, even though I didn't know that at the time. The goals I set, I achieved. I wanted two children, a boy and a girl, who would be well educated and feel at home in any cultural setting. This was important to both me and my husband who struggled as we lived in a mostly black environment and became educated in a mostly white one. I wanted to be well traveled and to write. At one time I dreamed of being a newspaper columnist, maybe even famous.

My major in college was journalism, after all. Ultimately, I basically went along for the ride. I took each day as it came and addressed life as it happened to me. I didn't have sense enough to know that I could have had more. Perhaps, I squandered gifts, like writing. I started a master's degree three times and never finished. I'm not sure I regret that. I'm not sure I regret anything.

I have two children, a boy and a girl. They are both college graduates living what I would define as successful and leading fulfilling lives. They are happy with their chosen careers and partners. I have a marriage of thirty-eight years and two grandchildren, whom I adore. Not everyone can make that claim. We've lived in seven different locations, Philadelphia, Pittsburgh, Washington DC, Baltimore, Boston, Connecticut and Houston, which afforded me and my family the opportunity to live in and learn about different life styles, people and sections of the country.

My family and I have traveled the world, including Asia and Europe. This brought my study of history alive for me. A serious career takes discipline and consistency, which I put into my home and never a job. Did I really need a career? Did I really want to be a writer or was my dream to be published? The publishing I have achieved several times over through articles I have written.

My mother was a stay at home wife, mother and community volunteer. What I have come to learn, these past thirty years, is that I really wanted my mother's life only with a bigger house and financial security. I'm there and I still have time.

# Sandra

## It's Been a Long Time Coming

I had a great time turning fifty…big party, lots of gifts! I thought by the time I turned fifty, professionally, I would be an educational administrator having a huge impact on students' lives. "Educator of the Year", I saw myself. They would make a movie about me and my experiences leading children up the ladder to success. Well, that didn't happen. Then when I joined corporate America, I imagined I would lead the corporate sales department at my company. After all, I was a really good sales rep, making the one hundred percent club every year for several years.

I wanted to teach new hires how to "sell". Well that didn't happen either. What did happen was decisions about my career life were made for me. My professional career was in the hands of others; managers who couldn't sell their way out of a paper bag. I had to listen to a thirty-something knit picking what I was doing. She herself, had never made all star, yet she felt the need to tell me, a seasoned marketer, how to sell. I found it difficult to adjust my attitude. And as the story goes, corporate America let me go. Me, the "all star", let go. After I made *them* all that money!

You play by the rules and then discover the rules don't mean anything. I went through the usual stages of grief, disbelief, pity, anger, rebound and then finally finding my own way. Now I'm doing exactly was I was born to do, give speeches about political issues I really believe in. And the good news is I get paid to do it. I can write and sign letters of protest without fear of retribution from my corporation. I don't have to be politically correct. My life is my own. Free at last at fifty. It was a long time coming, and I wouldn't change one step along the way. Each step has made me who I am today. I'm in a good place.

## Thank You For Letting Me Be Myself Again

Today, I'm comfortable doing what I choose, when I choose and with whom I choose. I've finally found a partner that "fits", fits my life and fits in my life. He doesn't tell me what to wear, where I can and cannot go. He doesn't notice if my fingernail polish matches my toes, a behavior I once mistook as loving attention. He is not the person I would have chosen twenty years ago. Things that were important to me then, aren't nearly as significant now. I've grown up and I finally recognize another grown up when I see one.

## Let's Get It On

I've discovered athletics in my later life though I'm disappointed that I'm not better at it. I'd love to run a marathon, except that goal will forever remain a "dream". At this point the knees couldn't take the stress. And what are we without dreams? Today, I have only one contemporary who shares my commitment to walking. While walking the lake front or in races we enter, we are often encouraged by the younger athletes to "stay the course, keep going, finish the race, for we've not far to go."

Though they may utter these words without malice in their hearts, I find them extremely annoying. What makes them think we can't finish the race? Why do they think we can't make it? What makes them assume that a little gray in the hair means less ability, less activity on our parts? They have no idea who the "old grey mare" is! I'm an unwilling participant in a youth-obsessed society. Since the change, I have no more cramps; no need for super absorbent pads; no bloating; PMS; cranky weeks or fear of pregnancy. Younger is not necessarily better, smarter or stronger. It's taken me thirty years to learn that.

# Maryann

## Who's That Lady?

They used to ask, "Who's that lady?" as I walked down the street in my twenties. A beautiful, svelte, can't touch this look, I was. I ate what I pleased with no consequences and took for granted a life-long confidence of perfection. Men loved me, women hated me. I couldn't get enough. I breezed into my thirties thinking to myself, what's the big deal? I have all the time in the world. I'll work out a little just to keep things firm and camera ready. Vitamins will help counter the poor diet intake on those on the run kind of days.

With a few unexpected changes, came the late thirties and early forties. The dry skin, I could moisturize. There were a few gray hairs around the temples. No problem, I can touch that up with color highlights. I vaguely noticed that as I aged that my bill at the beauty salon increased analogously. I experimented with a little Botox here and there just to freshen the look and lose a minor wrinkle here and there.

Did you know they have really good bras for raising those sagging breasts? They cost about eighty dollars and I have one in each color, white, black and nude. At fifty something, I've become better living through chemistry! I take Hydrochlorothiazide tablets for border-line high blood pressure and potassium to counteract their effects on the walking chemistry set that is my body. My hair is getting thinner while my waist is getting thicker. The minor workout of the thirties has become major in the fifties, walking, lifting weights, cardio workouts, kick boxing and spinning classes; water aerobics just to maintain and stop the weight gain that began in the forties.

Who am I? What have I become? I use lotion constantly on my neck and hands, which only softens the wrinkles, and does not erase them. My daily regimen now includes ginseng for memory; Actonel for bone loss; Glucosamine for joint pain; Zocor for high cholesterol. And I swear, if I don't get my daily dose of soy and Premarin to treat my menopausal symptoms, I might kill somebody! Gas escapes my body at will. All I have to do is bend over or reach from the front to the back seat of the car, and BAM, the fart is out. No warning, no expectation of release, I'm like a leaky valve.

As I approach sixty, "Who's that lady?" takes on a whole new meaning. I increased the Botox to raise my eyebrows. Now I look awake even when I'm asleep. I have no idea what the real color of my hair is. It ain't nothin' like I thought it would be.

# Elaine

## These Boots are Made for Walking

There's no time to waste. When I was forty I wondered what I would be doing at fifty. I knew I didn't want to be stuck in the same job I had. I thought about going back to school to be a lawyer. Except, who wants to be in school that long? Instead, I went back to become a psychologist. What an adjustment. The students were all younger than me and recent college graduates. What did they know of the real world?

I discovered that I was the same age as their parents. Gee that really helped us relate. One class was Personal and Professional Development. Only one other student and I were in our forties, old enough to understand the concept of personal and professional development. The twenty year olds were clueless. Personal development to them was snagging a dream date for the weekend, or maybe even accomplishing two dates with the same person within a month.

Eventually, we, the perceived old and wise, and they, the perceived young and stupid, formed a strange bond. We became friends. We elders were even invited to their future weddings. The young and stupid continued to constantly complain about the workload. What did they know? All they had to do was show up and do the academics. I was the only one who worked full-time and had a child. I finished my class work, wrote my dissertation and had a hysterectomy all while in grad school. The only one who could be called "Doctor" in the end was me. Boy, was I proud.

## What Will Be Will Be

There was one other male student in class with us who was fifty. He came to graduation dressed in a tux and roller skates. What a fun guy. His father had died young from a heart attack, so he was determined to get all his living in early. He never followed the rules even when he worked at the Cook County jail. Imagine the courage that must have taken.

He finished the program and then died, just like his father. He knew his fate. What a loss to us all. At forty, I thought I was going to die soon. Forty seemed so old. I felt old and tired. I guess because I had experienced a lot of life by then, more than planned. I had married and divorced, buried both parents, completed graduate school, raised my son and married him off. Fifty? That was just another day.

# Susan

## One Less Bell to Answer

Because I married young, by the time I divorced in my late thirties, I had a lot of catching up to do. Things most people did in their twenties, I starting doing in my forties and fifties. There were a lot of disco nights. My husband and I had never gone to clubs. We were too young and we were parents too soon also. I had never really dated either, so I had a lot to learn about relationships and expectations.

My official "youth" period began at the age of forty, experimenting with much that later resulted in my discovery that you can't repeat lost youth in midlife. It's just not the same. I was as square as the kitchen table and sexually inexperienced too. I didn't know sex could be so good. It had been rather "ho hum" in the marriage and that was all I knew. Fundamentally, I would like a serious relationship. However, the male attitudes, behaviors and general "BS" that I have encountered; most of which I would have been willing to overlook in my twenties, I will absolutely not tolerate at fifty.

Being unemployed and without your own car is a definite no, no. Living at home with your parents doesn't even get you a return phone call. And I'm not paying for dinner. I'd rather be alone.

I may never marry again and that's all right. I didn't expect at this moment in my life that I would not have be happily married. Then again, I didn't expect my feet would hurt like they do and I would need knee surgery either. I have led a healthy lifestyle and my body is still starting to fall apart. The deaths of friends and parents have made me aware of my own mortality. I'm not depressed by this, just more aware. I've gone full circle twice, so what's one more time or two? I have a lot of living still to do. I'm looking forward to the second half of my life and all its bittersweet possibilities.

# Linda

## Quicksand

Long before I turned fifty, I learned that what goes in, must be worked off. It has been a roller coaster ride, trying to control the "what goes in" part of the equation. I have a divine weakness for chocolate in any form, candy, cookies, cake, pie, liquid, solid, frozen. It doesn't matter. It's a daily requirement for life. I justify my habit by increased exercise. However, I find that the older I get, the less efficient my exercising becomes in maintaining that delicate balance.

My job requires me to travel, so I find myself, unfortunately, consuming airport food. The other day, while traveling through O'Hare airport in Chicago, I purchased a chicken fajita, which on the surface seemed innocent and healthy. It was chocked full of vegetables and wrapped in a whole-wheat tortilla. The problem was what came with the sandwich, a chocolate chip cookie. This was no ordinary cookie.

To begin with, it had real chunks of chocolate embedded in it. It was huge, about four inches in diameter. In fact it was called a quarter-pounder; like it was a hamburger or something. Anyway, at first bite, it was soft, chewy and chocolaty. In other words, just right, delicious. I plowed through half the cookie before deciding to look at the ingredients and caloric content. As suspected it was high in fat content, the bad kind and cholesterol and sodium. I knew this would be true which is probably why, subconsciously, I ate half of the cookie before checking.

Then I looked at the calories. At first glance, one hundred twenty calories seemed high, but not deadly. Then I noticed the servings. It said four per package. The package held one cookie. That could mean only one thing. I was about to devour a four hundred eighty calorie cookie. I prayed for the flight attendant to hurry along with the trash bag. Give me strength Lord! Let me get rid of the evidence; I mean temptation of that "throw it away before you kill yourself" cookie. In an instant, there she was with her little white baggy. I threw the cookie away, but not before taking one last bite. I know. I need help!

Epilogue

# At the End of the Day

# Arlene

## Function at the Junction

Our first girlfriend gathering was December 1996. A college class-mate decided to celebrate her fiftieth birthday at a spa resort in Wisconsin. She invited a few friends, who invited a few friends, one of whom called and invited me. I hadn't seen or talked with, except for a couple of women, these friends in thirty years, not even a Christmas card. The weekend was a blast. We caught up on old friends, past boy friends, marriages, divorces, children, jobs, moves, shared heartaches and political viewpoints. Most of us were teachers or at least started our initial careers as such. Some have moved on to corporate America or not-for-profit organizations.

Only women can cover thirty years in two nights. That's mainly because we engage in overlapping conversations, where everyone is talking at the same time. Miraculously, no comment goes unheard. Our first meeting was like a sister girl reunion. The second would be a "waiting to exhale" weekend at my home in Arizona where we have gathered every year since. Some years have been as small as six of us.

2006 was the biggest gathering yet, at twelve. Now, after ten years, we use any excuse to gather. We celebrate each of our birthdays throughout the year, take long walks along the Fox River, shop and sometimes just do lunch. Wherever we gather there is laughter, political discussion, an empathetic ear, advice whether solicited or not, support and celebration. It doesn't matter where we are, just as long as we're together. You can believe, wherever we gather, it's gonna be a "Function at the Junction".

## Ain't No Stopping Us Now

I am the sum of all my experiences. I have few regrets. Besides, there's no guarantee that decisions made differently would have produced a better result. If I had read more to my children would they have loved school more? If I had been more courageous and taken risks, would my professional or personal life have been more successful in some way? If I had the chance to do life over, I think that I would change very little.

At the end of the day, everything starts with you. You can't love and respect others until you first love and respect yourself. As you navigate the obstacle course called life, you are responsible for the choices made and paths taken. Everything in my life has not been as I dreamed, would have chosen or expected. I have learned some truths along the way from my parents and all the would-be parents who have taken an interest in me over the years.

These are fundamental truths shared in my life:

1. *Life's a dance. You learn as you go.*

   There are up cycles and down cycles in life and just like chapters in a book, when you finish one, TURN THE PAGE. Don't get stuck in the story.

2. *We carry with us all we have been.*

   We carry with us all we have been; the good, the bad and the ugly; all we have seen and done; all we still have yet to become. So don't let the bad and the ugly hold you back from the good that your future may yet hold for you.

3. *We should take no one in our lives for granted.*

   There are many people in our lives, I like to think, that serve a purpose whether it be immediately recognizable or not. Sometimes, the person you least expect, is there to say just what you need to hear. I've found that as I have navigated through my life, that relationships are at the center of everything that happens. Some cheer you on and some don't. Never let a misunderstanding or disagreement ruin a good relationship.

4. *It is important to keep your word.*

We are all connected and yet, the only person I have control over is me. I control my actions and my reactions to the things that happen to me. I have learned to embrace the good and release the not so good. I will forever be working on the release part. I know that nothing ruins a relationship faster than loss of trust. So I have led my life in a way to develop that expectation.

5. *We should live an honorable life.*

I believe one should do more than occupy space on earth. Throw yourself into life as someone who will make a difference. That doesn't always take money. We may not have all we want. Most often we have what we need.

6. *We can choose to be grateful.*

Our time on earth is very short. Moments are too precious to waste on regrets, yearning over things we may never have or worrying over things that may never happen. We can choose to be happy, despite our circumstance. Choose joy. We have options, more than our parents had.

7. *We must keep the faith.*

I have been blessed and I am grateful. I thank God for helping me climb mountains, face down obstacles and receive the blessings. More importantly, I've tried to share the blessings.

8. *Never forget your girlfriends.*

Girlfriends are not only your friends. They are also your sisters, your sisters-in-law, your daughters, sorors and other relatives too. They can come at any age or be any age. Some of my girlfriends I have known since kindergarten, others I met in college. They are more important as you get older. They give parties for you and your children when they graduate or get married, have babies, in whatever order that occurs.

Girlfriends are with you through good times and bad. They support you through bad relationships and marriages; love you even when they disagree with your choices. Love you even when you seem incapable of loving yourself; rejoice with you in happy times; laugh with you; cry with you.

Girlfriends help you find a new place to stay or even take you in when "it's time to go". They help you pack and unpack. Girlfriends are there for you when your parents pass away; children disappoint you; when you lose a job; men don't call; colleagues forget promises. They pray for you. No matter how many miles separate you or how much time passes between visits, girlfriends are always there for you. Life happens. Jobs and careers come and go. Children grow up and leave (hopefully). Parents die. Eventually, nature takes its course. Our bodies and minds start to fail.

When we start this journey called life, we have no idea how important friendships will be; no matter how much we love our husbands and children; no matter how wonderful they are. Girlfriends are a mainstay. So choose wisely!

When I was in grade school I had lots of "best" friends. Then as we moved on to junior high and high school, the concept of one best friend was introduced. This is a silly phase that girls go through while trying to find their identity, trying to fit in and trying to decide who to sit next to while traveling on the school bus to away football games. Probably, my cousin Cheryl was my best friend growing up. Cheryl and I were the same age and because of that she was the person closest to me; with whom I spent most of my free time; the one who held my secrets.

She would hold that position until after the teen years when my little sister finally "grew up". We are actually quite different today. Best friends change as we grow up, as situations change, as circumstances change. What we really have is a circle of friends. Some are part of your social life, your work life, your spiritual life, your community life, your academic life, your family life. And some are just *meant to be.*

## A New Day is Dawning, There's Plenty of Light

Now as we turn sixty and start to retire, we have more and less time with each other, all at once, as we start to "scatter" to be near the kids; near the grandkids; back home; to states in the sun. We can take more time to enjoy ordinary things in life. The pressures of work, deadlines are gone.

The life as chauffer to the children's daily activities is over. We are free to be who we are and not who we need to be. We are not old. We are simply no longer young. We reflect on the lives we have led. Have we saved enough, made wise financial investments? Did we fulfill our purpose? Did we accomplish all we thought we would? All we said we would? Who cares!

No more fear of failure for now it is done. We can see clearly now. There is no more sense of urgency. Monday is just another day. As is Friday. It has been a good run and besides it's not over yet. There ain't no stopping us now. We still have contributions to make, hills to conquer. We are freed from what we "need to do" and available to do what we want to do. We have time now, time and money. We can indulge ourselves in facials, manicures, pedicures and massages.

We can take long walks and sip our coffee over extended talks. At the beginning of this book I said I didn't know Jack. This is what I do know. This *is* the house that *Jack* built. But I own it. Now turn off the lights.

# About the Author

## Arlene Yvonne Avery Burke

Arlene Burke was born in Evanston, Illinois where she attended Evanston Public Schools, graduating from Evanston Township High School in 1964. She holds a bachelor in elementary and special education from Northern Illinois University and a master's degree from Northeastern Illinois University and Purdue University in Learning Disabilities and Educational Administration. She has been married to Sterling M. Burke since 1969 and is the mother of two children.

Ms. Burke taught fifth grade and special education students at the middle and high school levels in Evanston, Illinois, Matteson, Illinois and Cobb County, Georgia for seventeen years. She also worked as a consultant and supervisor with the Chicago Regional Program Chapter I serving the needs of students and teachers in non-public educational institutions for severely handicapped clients. Ms. Burke's career continued for another eighteen years as a Senior Client Representative and Educational Consultant in the IBM Midwestern Education Industry Unit where she earned numerous marketing excellence awards. Until she retired in December 2005, she was responsible for marketing to and consulting with schools and colleges in the IBM central region to help bring about technology based systemic change.

Ms. Burke has also been active in community organizations such as the Olympia Fields Enhancement Organization, Jack and Jill of America and currently serves as Chairperson of the Olympia Fields Beautification Committee. She was elected a Monee Township Trustee and served for three years. As a member of the South Suburban Chicago Chapter of The Links, Incorporated, she has held the offices of Secretary, Vice President and President. She has been a member of Delta Sigma Theta Public Service Sorority for over forty years. Additionally, both her mother and sister are members of this sisterhood.

Ms. Burke has lived in Evanston, University Park, Flossmoor and Olympia Fields in Illinois, Pensacola, Florida and Roswell Georgia. She and her husband presently enjoy part time residence in Chandler, Arizona.

# Order Form

Mail Checks or Money Orders to:

Arlene Y. Avery Burke / emersonstreet books
20185 Augusta Drive
Olympia Fields, Illinois 60461
Phone: 1-708-256-2348
Fax: 1-708-748-8531
e-mail: ayburke@emersonstreetbooks.com

Please send ___ copy(ies) of *Nothin Like I Thought* to:

Name: _____

Address:_____

City:_____State: _____Zip:_____

Telephone: (____)_____/ (____)_____

Email: _____

I have enclosed $15.95, plus $6.00 shipping per book for a total of $_____.

Sales Tax: Add 7.75% to total cost of books for orders shipped to IL addresses.

For Bulk or Wholesale Rates, Call: 1-708-256-2348

Or email: *ayburke@emersonstreetbooks.com*

Please visit: www.emersonstreetbooks.com